MAD KINGS & QUEENS

History's Most Famous Raving Royals

Library of Congress Cataloging-in-Publication Data Available

1 2 3 4 5 6 7 8 9 10

Published in 2008 by Sterling Publishing Co., Inc.
387 Park Avenue South, New York, NY 10016

Copyright © 2007 JW Cappelens Forlag under license from Gusto Company AS
Written by Alison Rattle & Allison Vale
Original concept by Gusto Company
Designed by Allen Boe
Illustrations, ScanPix

Distributed in Canada by Sterling Publishing
c/o Canadian Manda Group, 165 Dufferin Street
Toronto, Ontario, Canada M6K 3h6

For information about custom editions, special sales, premium and corporate purchases,
please contact Sterling Special Sales Department at 800-805-5489 or specialsales@
sterlingpub.com

Manufactured in China

Sterling ISBN: 978-1-4027-6306-9

MAD KINGS & QUEENS

History's Most Famous Raving Royals

Alison Rattle & Allison Vale

STERLING

New York / London
www.sterlingpublishing.com

Contents

INTRODUCTION

They don't come more appalling than aristocrats. During the last five hundred years of European monarchy, the royal courts and palaces have seethed with rulers who have been, at best, eccentric or mentally deficient, and at worst, psychopathic monsters who have committed the most heinous acts while sheltered behind the cloak and crown of royalty.

Some have slaughtered, slashed, tortured, and murdered their way through their ruthless and bloody reigns. A handful extended the boundaries of human depravity.

The proliferation of inbreeding among royal families, as documented in Appendix II, spawned a tragic historical heritage of simpletons, "sad-heads," and hideously deformed imbeciles, all laughingly given powers beyond their comprehension. The certifiably deranged royalty in this peculiar catalogue all have one thing in common: they lacked a compulsion to "keep up appearances."

This book examines and delves into the lives and minds of forty of the most controversial, misguided, and deplorable royals from Europe's last seven hundred years. It provides revealing insights into the scandalous, whimsical, lunatic, and nefarious exploits committed by the most idiosyncratic rulers the world has ever seen. From a duchess who bathed in the blood of virgins and a prince who gleefully impaled tens of thousands, to a king who collected tall soldiers and an empress who cut out tongues, we confront the raving rulers of history who, even today, remain a compelling and disturbing reminder of the lethal combination of irrationality and absolute power.

ISABELLA "SHE-WOLF" OF FRANCE

(c.1295–1358)

I sabella was born into the French royal family and married the King of England. Her reign could have been remarkable, but her husband's homosexuality, encroaching mental instability, and poor judgment fueled her considerable rage and ambition and sealed the fate of all who stood in her way. She has gone down in history as a callous and hard-hearted woman who was so hungry for power and bloody revenge that she was driven to regicide, earning her the title, She-Wolf of France.

A fine romance

Isabella was the daughter of the King of France, and had been raised from infancy to expect a politically expedient marriage and a future abroad. She had been betrothed to England's Prince Edward, who was ten years her senior, since she was seven, and by her twelfth birthday, the Pope had already been urging their families to tie the knot for some years.

When Isabella and her new husband arrived on English soil, they were greeted by his lover, Piers Gaveston, who was bedecked with the priceless jewels that Isabella's father had given Edward as a wedding gift. It was a defining moment in her relationship with her husband and, not surprisingly, Isabella took an instant dislike to Gaveston.

Edward and Gaveston had been lovers since adolescence. Once Edward took the throne as King Edward II, he opened the King's coffers to Gaveston and lavished affection upon him, to the virtual exclusion of the Queen. Isabella grew despondent, and wrote achingly bleak letters back home in which she despaired of her marriage and bemoaned her empty marital bed.

Initially, she bore her burden well. But not so the archbishops and the barons, who grew so irritated by the financial burden of her husband's flirtations that they raised armies and went on the offensive. With Gaveston and a pregnant Isabella in tow, Edward fled to Scotland where he hoped to find refuge. He didn't. As the hostile armies approached, a terrified Edward grabbed his lover and together they fled, leaving Isabella, pregnant and alone, to escape the wrath of the advancing Scottish King, Robert I, the Bruce. It was an unforgivable act of betrayal that was thereafter to color Isabella's every action, even after Gaveston's death in 1312.

A lover and a plot

Isabella eventually fled to the court of her brother, King Charles IV, in France. There, she fell hopelessly in love with a Welshman, Roger Mortimer. Mortimer and Isabella raised an army, borrowed a flotilla of warships, and marched on Edward, rallying support as they went. Victorious, Isabella ruthlessly ordered the gruesome execution of any of the King's allies, and tortures for those Isabella accused of sodomy with her husband that included disembowelment and castration.

Isabella subjected Edward to a humiliating public de-frocking, and broadcasted that he was no longer suitable to reign because of his mental deficiencies. She then had him unceremoniously incarcerated.

She hoped to remove any threat from the overthrown monarch permanently, and tried to hasten Edward's death with starvation and torture. As an additional measure, she had Edward placed in a cell above the castle morgue, so that the foul stench of rotting corpses filled the air he breathed. But Edward proved more hardy than expected, and after eight months was still alive.

Regicide

Nervous that the longer he survived the greater the risk an army would be raised in his name, Isabella grew impatient. In a move that would ensure her eternal infamy, she ordered that fifteen men enter his prison cell in the dead of night and carry out his execution. The King had a red-hot spit inserted into his back passage and died screaming in agony.

Imprisonment and mental collapse

In place of Edward II, Isabella's son was crowned King as soon as he came of age, following a brief period of her regency. Edward III neither forgot nor forgave his mother's part in the assassination of his father. He had Mortimer executed and ordered his mother to be incarcerated in Castle Rising in Norfolk, with orders that she was never to show her face in public again. Inventories show that King Edward III ensured his mother lived in some comfort, but he held firm to the terms of her imprisonment. She even had to travel a twelve-mile round trip through underground tunnels to pray at Chapel.

Her incarceration lasted for nearly thirty years. Alone with her thoughts for such an extended period, she grew increasingly unstable. The loss of her title, her lover, and her uneasy conscience conspired to undermine her mental health. Legend has it that, in her latter years, she roamed the castle ramparts under the cover of darkness, wailing and moaning like a crazed she-wolf.

JOAN I OF NAPLES

(1326–1382)

J oan was a fiery and headstrong young woman who asserted her will over heads of state, European monarchs, and the papacy. No institution could withstand her ambitions: not politics, the law, or the Church. Though her intractability may not conform to any modern definition of insanity, she was an unconventional individual, both potent and formidable; rare qualities for a woman of her time.

An early start

She was born Joanna, granddaughter of the King of Naples. At age seven she was betrothed to her six-year-old cousin, Andrew, of Hungary. At sixteen, when her grandfather died, she inherited the throne, but was outraged to learn that her grandfather's will had designated Andrew to rule Naples on equal terms with her. She kicked up such a fuss that the Pope sent a cardinal to investigate. Such was her influence that the cardinal quashed the will and Joanna was crowned Joan I of Naples.

Inauspicious marriage prospects

It was not enough for Joan to seize the monarchy from her cousin and enrage her Hungarian in-laws: she is also alleged to have made two attempts on Andrew's life. The first, to be staged as a mock hunting accident, was thwarted. The second was successful: in his private chambers in the Castle of Aversa, Andrew was beckoned out on urgent business, and as he hurried to attend, he was jumped by a hidden assailant, strangled with a rope, and thrown from the window.

Joan's persistent reluctance to investigate Andrew's death raised suspicion against her. The Vatican was called to lead the inquiry, but her name was never cleared. From that point on she lived in permanent fear of a Hungarian reprisal.

An eye for profit

Joan tried to maintain a pious facade in the face of mounting papal and public disapproval. However, in 1347, she opened a state-run brothel, which she called "The Abbey," in Avignon. It was designed much as a convent or a monastery would have been: the women were required to attend daily religious services and were not available for trade on Sundays or at Easter. Clients were strictly Christian and aristocratic, and would retire to the women's rooms in their cloisters. But there was no disguising the fact that money changed hands in return for sexual favors. However much Joan dressed up the establishment as noble, Christian, and respectable, it was nevertheless a whorehouse.

Unlucky in love and in business

Joan remarried another three times after Andrew's death, and twice was made a widow. She continued to make a stand against the Hungarians, albeit from the relative safety of France.

When a papal dispute in the late 1370s caused a schism and, bizarrely, the co-existence of both a Pope and an "Antipope," Joan backed the papal rival and lost. This put her in the uncomfortable position of having incurred the wrath of both the powerful Hungarian dynasty and the mighty Vatican.

Miserable end

Joan's reign had made her too many enemies for it to end well. After the resolution of the papal schism, the victorious Pope Urban VI removed her from the throne of Naples in favor of the more sympathetic and malleable Charles III. Forced to surrender the monarchy, Joan was imprisoned, wretched and defeated. She was strangled to death in her cell in 1382.

ROBERT III OF SCOTLAND

(c.1340–1406)

I n contrast to most other mad monarchs, there was nothing despotic about Robert III of Scotland. He was a gentle, timid man who suffered injuries in a riding accident that left him permanently frail, both physically and mentally. In his bewildered disquiet, he abandoned two of his sons, one to a lingering death in a dungeon, and the other, an eleven-year-old, on a rugged Scottish island.

Inauspicious birthright

Robert's early years were hardly the auspicious start a future king would wish for. His parents were so closely related that they had to seek a special papal dispensation to legitimize their marriage; at the time, Robert was already ten years old. Matters didn't ever really improve. When he came to the throne, he was already crippled and fifty years old. His self-esteem was so low that he couldn't bring himself to assume his own name as his royal title: he considered that his Christian name, John, had proved unlucky in the past, and took instead the name of his father, Robert II.

Chaos

As King, Robert wallowed in depression. He withdrew increasingly from public life, abandoning all semblance of rulership. Before long, he became a hopeless recluse.

Unable to assert himself with that degree of ruthlessness necessary for a Scottish king (at a time when the tension between the highlands and the lowlands was growing pronounced), Robert was happy to hand over rulership to his brother, the Earl of Fife, later retitled the Duke of Albany. He didn't put up any resistance when his brother announced to all that King Robert III was unfit to govern.

James I of Scotland

Before she died, his wife persuaded Robert to give his eldest son a dukedom, making him David, Duke of Rothesay, at which point he also took over as Governor. David was rash and impetuous, and consequently he enjoyed neither success nor widespread support.

Albany arrested David and had him imprisoned in the dungeons at Albany's castle. There, Robert's son was literally abandoned and left to starve to death.

An island sanctuary for his son

David's death, at least, elicited some reaction from the now widowed and terrified king. Fearing that his other son, James, would suffer a similar fate, he had him shipped off to France. But before James could board the ship, Albany's men attacked, fighting to capture the Prince, and Robert ordered that his son be rowed to safety. Sanctuary came in the form of a tiny, rocky, wind- and sea-battered island, known as Bass Rock, where eleven-year-old James was effectively abandoned for a month or more, with no shelter and no word of rescue.

When he was finally placed on board a merchant ship headed for France, the unhappy Prince was captured by pirates and eventually imprisoned by the English King in the Tower of London, where he languished for eighteen years.

The end

James's capture was the final straw for the ailing Robert. Deeply insecure and crushed by the burden of his disastrous reign, his depression took its final hold. He refused food and water, which helped to hasten his decline. Before he died, Robert announced that he was not fit to be buried alongside other Scottish Kings; he felt too unworthy, and requested that his final resting place be a dunghill. He asked that his epitaph read: *Here lies the worst of kings and the most miserable of men.*

CHARLES VI OF FRANCE

(1368–1422)

During the early part of his reign, when he was popular with his subjects, Charles VI of France earned the nickname "Charles the Well-Beloved" (*Charles le Bien-Aimé*). However, his later bouts of psychosis led to his renaming as "Charles the Mad" (*Charles le Fol*).

The early years

He was born in Paris, the son of French monarch Charles V. His mother, Jeanne de Bourbon, was mentally unstable, as were her father and brother. Charles's mother suffered a complete nervous breakdown when he was very young. He was crowned King of France in 1380, although for the first eight years his uncle, Philip the Bold, was the effective ruler.

Where did it all go wrong?

Charles appears to have experienced his first fit of madness in his mid-twenties, following a freak illness which made his hair and fingernails fall out. This coincided with the attempted murder of his friend and advisor, Olivier de Clisson. Charles, still feverish and incoherent from his illness, set off to Brittany with an army to track down the culprits. On the journey he was traveling through a forest when he was approached by an unkempt man who warned the king that he had been betrayed and pleaded with him to turn back. Startled by a fallen lance dropped by his page, Charles went crazy and killed four of his own soldiers before he could be stopped.

He lay on the ground in a catatonic state for several minutes and had had to be transported back home in a cart, where he remained in a coma for two days. When he regained consciousness he was full of remorse, but this signaled the start of mental health problems that would plague him for the rest of his life.

The Ball of Burning Men

In January of the following year, a bizarre accident further damaged Charles's frail psyche. His wife, Bavarian princess Isabeau, gave a masked ball where Charles and a group of his courtiers dressed up as wild men and danced around chained to each other. One of the courtiers came too close to a lighted torch and caught fire. The King was saved from burning to death by the quick thinking of the Duchesse de Berry, who smothered him with her dress, but four of the other revelers were killed. The accident became known as the *Bal des Ardents* ("the Ball of Burning Men"). Deeply affected by this, Charles suffered another wave of insanity the following summer. The royal physician performed trepanning on the King (drilling a hole in his skull), but after a temporary improvement his condition worsened. At one point, when he began fiercely attacking anyone who entered his quarters, he was even subjected to an exorcism.

The glass king

During one of his many bouts of madness Charles became convinced that he was made of glass and that if he fell or was knocked over he would shatter. So he instructed his tailors to sew iron rods into his clothing for protection.

A lame legacy

By the time of his death from a brief illness Charles had lost his wife to a succession of suitors and his inept rule had so enfeebled the body politic that England's Henry V invaded and easily defeated France, even though his army was outnumbered five to one. Charles was compelled to recognize Henry as his successor, repudiate the legitimacy of his son, the dauphin, and give the hand of his daughter Catherine in marriage to Henry.

ISABEL OF PORTUGAL

(1428–1496)

I sabel of Portugal was a beautiful young princess who fell in love with a king, but her marriage was tainted by her obsessive behavior, her madly possessive nature, and her chronic depression. She ended her days widowed and alone, hidden away in a bleak tower.

Keeping it in the family

Isabel may have inherited not only her good looks, but also her incipient mental instability. Her father, Prince Joao, married his illegitimate brother's daughter, Isabella of Braganza, who was to become Isabel's mother. Close family ties of this kind may have brought to the surface problems that lurked subclinically in the bloodlines of many European monarchs.

The King's favorite, the Queen's adversary

In 1447, King Juan II of Castile, a widower in his early forties, was keen to find himself an eligible young bride. Alvaro de Luna, the King's closest

confidant since childhood, steered King Juan in the direction of the captivating teenage beauty Isabel, unwittingly sealing his own fate. Juan was immediately entranced, and wasted no time proposing marriage.

Isabel was soon to discover the extent of her husband's reliance upon Alvaro. Alvaro advised when the royal couple should consummate their marriage, and how frequently and upon which occasions they should bed each other. Isabel became jealous and possessive, her insecurities stoked by her husband's devotion to another man. Alvaro's interference in their sex life drove her into alternating bouts of melancholia and rage. Her mental instability became more prominent in these early years of marriage.

Postnatal depression

In April of 1451, the King and Queen gave birth to their first child, a daughter, whom they named Isabel. This joyful experience only seemed to aggravate Isabel's depressive tendencies. She began to demonstrate her inclination towards reclusive isolation, which would prove to be the pattern for the rest of her life.

Isabel secreted herself away in her apartments, spending her days alone, motionless and mute, except when in the presence of her husband. Her fears about Alvaro grew more and more fanatical and became the focus of Isabel's frenzied and furious rages. Finally, worn down by his wife's bouts of madness, King Juan acquiesced in a plot to oust Alvaro from the royal favor. Alvaro was arrested and executed in 1453.

The mad woman in the tower

King Juan never recovered from Alvaro's death. Although Isabel gave birth to a son, Alfonso, later the same year, Juan weakened and died in 1454. Isabel, although only twenty-six years old, was now a widow.

Henry, Juan's son by his first wife, was summoned to assume the monarchy. No longer on the throne, Isabel was moved to the tower of a grim castle, where her previous experience of royal grandeur was nothing but a distant memory. She remained obsessively true to her late husband, refusing even to be alone in male company.

Isabel's children, who initially lived in her care, were deemed to be increasingly at risk as the mental health of their mother grew ever weaker. They were removed to a convent to complete their schooling, and later were requested to return to the royal court. Now deprived of the company of her children, Isabel's depression intensified. She became increasingly disturbed, troubled by disembodied and ghostly voices. Her haunting paranoia infected all aspects of her consciousness, and eventually she would receive visits from her children only if her face was hidden.

When her daughter visited her on her deathbed, Isabel had long since ceased to recognize her child. She had spent the last forty-two years of her life in the tower, wretched and alone.

VLAD "THE IMPALER" OF WALACHIA

(c.1431–1476)

T he inspiration for Bram Stoker's famous vampire, Count Dracula, Vlad the Impaler may not have drunk blood, but he was certainly one of the most appallingly cruel, wild, and bloodthirsty tyrants to have ever stalked through the annals of history.

Early life

Raised to be a conventional prince, Vlad was an exceptional warrior, horseman, and scholar: he was fluent in several languages as well as the art of etiquette. His father had sworn to uphold an allegiance to fight the Turks, and was honored with membership in a secret society known as the Order of the Dragon, or Dracul. Thus Vlad earned his famous title, Dracula—"Son of the Dragon." At the age of eleven, Vlad and his younger brother, Radu, were taken hostage and held at the palace of a Turkish sultan. Here Vlad lived under a constant threat of death, and the experience seems to have marked him for the rest of his life.

Vlad "The Impaler" of Walachia

Grasping power

Following the death of his father, and years of exile, Vlad returned to his homeland of Walachia and seized control of the throne. Determined to assert his power, he invited all the noble families of Walachia—the "Boyar"—to a banquet. Vlad suspected that many of them had betrayed his father and brother. Once the feast was over, the old and infirm were impaled on wooden stakes. The younger and sturdier were enslaved and put to work building him a castle. A short time later, he gathered together the beggars of the region, boarded them up in a great hall, and burned them to death. His reasoning? "I did this so no one would be poor in my realm."

Reign of unspeakable torments

Vlad controlled his subjects with a blood-soaked fist, and anyone who opposed his rule or who committed even minor crimes, was subjected to gruesome and agonizing death. Adulterous wives, cheating merchants, even one poor woman who had sewn her husband's shirt too short—all were killed in the most hideous manner. Vlad's preferred method of execution was to impale his victims. He turned this torture into an art form, arranging the stakes and the victims into complex patterns, with some bodies impaled upright, and others upside down. The wooden stakes, plunged from the anus to the mouth, were smoothed and oiled at the tip to ease the passage through the body and avoid damaging vital organs. This ensured an agonizingly slow death. Victims of noble birth were given longer stakes, so as to be higher from the ground, and were often first invited to dine with Vlad, surrounded by rotting staked corpses. No one was safe from Vlad's bloodthirsty wrath. Even mothers with babes at the breast were impaled together. Vlad was also partial to other forms of torture, and thought nothing of boiling people alive, skinning, scalping, and mutilating, or roasting children and feeding them to their mothers. All in all, this maniacal ruler managed to dispose of at least one-tenth of his citizens.

The forest of the impaled

In 1462, when the Turks invaded Walachia, they were totally unprepared for the sickening sight which met them on the outskirts of the capital city, Tirgoviste: rows upon rows of large stakes upon which the rotting bodies of at least 20,000 men, women, and children hung. The horror was enough to make the army bolt in fear.

Among the rats

When the Turks finally invaded, Vlad fled to Hungary where he was kept under house arrest for several years. His thirst for torture appears not to have diminished during his incarceration, and he turned his attentions to the only victims he had access to. His room soon became littered with the impaled carcasses of rats, mice, and birds. Vlad was reinstated as King of Wallachia upon his release from prison in 1468. He died in 1476, reportedly, the victim of an assassination. His decapitated body was buried in an unmarked grave; it is said that his head was never found.

JUANA OF CASTILE

(1479–1555)

Queen Juana I of Castile was highly-strung and physically addicted to her dashing but adulterous husband, Philip the Handsome of Austria. Her passionate ardor was to grow wildly out of control, leading to profound jealousy, mental instability, and deranged antics that earned her the title "Juana la Loca" (Joanna the Mad).

Early days

As a child, Juana was sullen, moody, and solitary. Some interpreted her reclusive and haughty behavior as the hallmarks of natural majestic dignity, but those close to her were disturbed to recognize in her moods a resemblance to her grandmother, the mad Queen Isabel of Portugal. At the age of sixteen, and on the brink of her sexual awakening, Juana was shipped off to Flanders to marry the only son of the Emperor Maximilian I, the tall, dark, and insatiably virile Philip the Handsome. By all reports, the couple were instantly attracted to one another and enjoyed an actively carnal relationship.

A marriage made in hell

The passion soon grew one-sided however, with Philip reverting to his bachelor pastimes of feasting, drinking, and bed-hopping. Juana, incensed by his unfaithfulness, flew into uncontrollable rages, spending nights pounding on the walls of her lonely bedchamber. Philip refused to countenance her behavior, and punished her further by withdrawing all conjugal visits. Sexually frustrated and increasingly unbalanced, Juana grew more hysterical as her desire for her husband intensified.

Following the deaths of her elder brother and sister, Juana returned to Spain as heiress, taking Philip with her. On receiving a cold welcome from her mother, and with a husband desperate to return to Flanders and his bevy of mistresses, the pregnant Juana sunk further into despondency and irrationality. She lashed out at servants, kicking, screaming, and biting, and she hurled heinous insults. Her family locked the deranged Juana in the Castle of La Mota and her philandering husband returned to Flanders without her.

Witchcraft and sorcery

Imprisoned and pining for her husband, Juana's obsession grew to extravagant proportions. After giving birth to her fourth child, Ferdinand, she managed to make her way back to Flanders, leaving her son behind. She arrived home to find a mistress at her husband's side. Juana attacked brutally, hacking the woman's hair off in public. Desperate to regain her husband's affections, Juana turned to sorcery, spending days locked in her rooms concocting ineffective love potions.

Coffin canoodling

Juana's mother, Isabella I of Castile, died in November of 1504, leaving Juana to take on the mantle of Queen of Castile. Pregnant once more, the new queen traveled back to Spain to claim her inheritance, taking the irascible Philip with her. Whether he was poisoned or struck down by a mysterious illness is uncertain, but Philip died suddenly, leaving the pregnant queen in a state of inconsolable grief. The lovestruck queen refused to be parted from her husband's body and several times after he was entombed had his coffin opened to view his remains. When she fled the town of Burgos for Torquemada to escape a plague, she brought Philip's coffin with her, and when she opened the coffin to ensure he was still in it, she began to kiss and caress his rotting corpse. When her daughter Catarina was born, Juana seized upon her as the final reminder of her beloved husband and guarded the child jealously from a locked room in the castle of Tordesillas.

Juana was ultimately declared incapable of assuming the monarchy, and her father and oldest son both ruled in her stead. When her son saw her in a state of disrepair in her castle, he advised that she should never be allowed to be seen publicly again. Although nominally the monarch of Spain, she languished alone in her castle tower for nearly forty years.

HENRY VIII OF ENGLAND

(1491–1547)

H enry VIII was arrogant on a scale that can only be tolerated for an absolute monarch. He treated any constraints of the law with disdain, overturning those he could, and beheading anyone who attempted to stand in his way. He approached life with an unrestrained excess that extended to his obsessive compulsion to sire a healthy male heir.

Early years

Henry VIII had not been raised to be King. His father, Henry VII, had witnessed brother fight brother throughout the Wars of the Roses and in an effort to reduce the risk of the same happening to his sons, he groomed his firstborn son, Arthur, for kingship, and his second son, Henry, for a religious life. Arthur's early death changed everything. In particular, it changed Henry VII's parenting. He became protective in the extreme toward his only surviving son, keeping him close, restricting his freedoms, and limiting his opportunities. The wild excesses of his adulthood may well have been Henry's response to his stifled adolescence.

Power-crazed

In the early fifteenth century, there was little to hinder any king's claim to absolute supremacy in all things. Among Christian nations, only the Pope as head of the Church had any decisive influence. Henry VIII was a headstrong monarch, and he saw any decree of the Pope that countermanded his authority as an intolerable impediment. His reign is remembered for the dissolution of the monasteries, the creation of the Protestant Church of England, and the instatement of the English monarch as "Defender of the Faith."

Any who challenged the King's exalted status of Head of the Church were charged with treason and executed.

It wasn't only the Church that felt the wrath of King Henry. Though he indulged freely in sexual excesses and compulsive gambling, he found some practices so insufferable that he legislated against them. He abhorred sodomy sufficiently to make it a capital offence for the first time in English history; likewise the practice of witchcraft.

He imposed additional dictatorial restrictions upon his subjects, limiting their freedom of speech by making the speaking or printing of any dissent punishable by death. His autocratic reign brought the British monarchy closer to absolute power than ever before.

The "King's Great Matter"

The delicate question of how Henry could rid himself of one wife so that he could be free to remarry was known about court as the "King's Great Matter." It became a political flashpoint when Henry gave up all hopes that his first wife, Catherine of Aragon, would ever give birth to a son. He sought papal dispensation to get the marriage annulled, and was prepared to twist the truth significantly in order to make sure it happened. When Henry forged ahead with his second marriage, the Pope declared it null and void and excommunicated him. Henry responded by breaking with Rome and establishing the Church of England, of which he was the Supreme Head.

Henry's second wife, Anne Boleyn, gave birth to Elizabeth, future Queen of England, but her failure to provide him with a son led to her being accused of a vast array of trumped up charges ranging from witchcraft, incest, and adultery, to inflicting injury upon His Royal Highness. She was charged with treason and beheaded.

Wife number three, Jane Seymour, died shortly after giving birth to a son, Edward VI. Henry mourned quickly and set about selecting wife number four.

After some great effort, Henry was persuaded to marry Anne of Cleves. She was plain and pockmarked and, as it turned out, not at all to Hen-

HENRY VIII OF ENGLAND

ry's liking. Nevertheless, when the time came, she was canny enough to insist the marriage had never been consummated, claiming the royal couple had simply met nightly to kiss platonically upon the forehead. The marriage was painlessly annulled.

Wife number five, Catherine Howard, seemed a good partner for Henry until she foolishly indulged in an extramarital affair. Henry, with the help of an act of Parliament making it a treasonable offense for a King's wife to be unchaste, had yet another marriage annulled, shortly before Catherine Howard's beheading.

Wife number six, Catherine Parr, outlived Henry and persuaded him to reinstate his daughters, Mary and Elizabeth, into the line of succession.

A sick and portly end

Henry's excesses took their toll. His overeating, alcoholic binges, and sexual escapades all contributed to his death at age fifty-five. All three of his children sat on the throne, but ironically it was his daughter, Elizabeth, who served the longest and most memorably.

IVAN "THE TERRIBLE" OF RUSSIA

(1530–1584)

I van IV Vasilyevich was the first ruler of Russia to call himself "Tsar" or Emperor King. His name is synonymous with torture, cruelty, and paranoia. He established a bodyguard, the Oprichniki, which has been described as Russia's first "secret police." Nevertheless, many people in Russia consider him a national hero.

The early years

When Ivan was three years old his father died and his mother, Jelena Glinskaya, became regent until she was poisoned five years later by nobles at court. Ivan was very intelligent and one of the most literate of Russian rulers. However, after his beloved nurse, Agrafena, was sent to a nunnery, his childhood became one of loneliness and neglect. He and his deaf-mute brother, Yuri, often went hungry; they also witnessed murders and were subject to beatings and verbal abuse.

By the time Ivan was in his teens it was clear that he was deeply disturbed. One of his favorite pastimes was throwing live animals from towers and watching them fall to their painful deaths. He tore feathers off live birds, poked out their eyes, and cut them open for sport. He also raped, robbed, and killed villagers.

The first Tsar

Ivan was crowned Russia's first Tsar when he was seventeen. He married soon afterwards, following a national competition to find a bride. Virgins from all over the kingdom were assembled in the Kremlin for his inspection. He chose Anastasia Romonovna, who seems to have made him happy and quelled his troubled spirit, until her sudden death in 1560. Ivan was convinced she had been poisoned. After losing the love of his life he degenerated into a psychopathic tyrant.

He married eight times, and each of his unfortunate wives was either poisoned or made to become a nun.

The Oprichniki

These personal bodyguards were a ruthless militia which Ivan clothed in monks' garb. They went to any length to protect God's Tsar and raped, tortured, and murdered thousands as they terrorized the country. Ivan personally devised ever more ingenious and devious tortures, inspired by the Bible and interpretations of Hell. Victims were impaled, roasted on spits, or fried in huge skillets. He tortured and butchered all sixty thousand inhabitants of the city of Novgorod during a week-long orgy in 1570.

Ivan the repentant

In 1581 Ivan stabbed his eldest son (and heir) in a fit of violent rage during an argument. He was filled with remorse and took up monastic orders in an attempt to save his soul. He posthumously pardoned all those whom he had executed and before his death he was re-christened as the monk, Jonah. He was buried in his monk's habit, leaving his mentally subnormal son, Fyodor, to end the family dynasty.

ERIK XIV OF SWEDEN

(1533–1577)

E rik XIV of Sweden was a king paralyzed by personal insecurity. He surrounded himself with outlandish grandeur and opulence, and in an attempt to mask his inferiority complex, was the first Swedish monarch to insist upon being addressed as "Majesty." Erik's paranoid fear of the nobility who served him contributed to his unstable mental condition and eventual insanity.

The early years

Erik was born at the Royal Castle in Stockholm, the eldest son of Gustav I and Catherine of Saxe-Lauenburg (who died before Erik was two). Erik's father, although remembered as a shrewd and able king, was also possessed of a violent and prodigious temper: he is reported to have torn out his daughter's hair by the roots and beat to death a goldsmith whose only crime had been to take a day off work without permission. Although Erik bore witness to his father's terrible rages, he himself grew to be a young man of intelligence and great artistic capability.

He surrounded himself with a band of well-educated friends whom his father detested and labeled "a group of toads." A desire to live up to his father's great name and to build upon his own fragilities drove Erik to make a number of unsuccessful marriage proposals to politically influential women, such as Renata of Lorraine, Mary I of Scotland, and Elizabeth I of England (whom Erik was on his way to woo when news of his father's death reached him).

A growing paranoia

Crowned King in 1560, Erik's mental condition, which was fragile at best, soon cracked. He failed to secure the hand of a number of aristocratic women through his own fickleness, and eventually married a common jailer's daughter. His growing paranoia led him to believe he was being laughed at and ridiculed for his choice of bride. Like his father before him, Erik flew into rages for the most inconsequential of reasons. Anyone unfortunate enough to be caught smiling, whispering, or coughing in his presence was likely to be sentenced to death for their presumed treasonous plotting. Many innocents were put to the sword for "annoying the King."

The Sture murders

In 1566, Erik's fear of aristocratic families drove him to arrest and condemn to death for gross neglect of duty the young Count Nils, a prominent member of the ancient and influential Sture family. The charges were completely fabricated. A number of other members of the Sture family were systematically murdered. Nils Sture met his death at the hands of Erik himself, who visited the cell where Nils was held and stabbed him in a violent frenzy. Shortly after, Erik suffered from a bout of remorse and arranged a substantial and extravagant funeral for the Stures.

The end

Erik's grip on reality gradually diminished. He spent long periods of time in a confused and depressed state. At one point he lost all sense of himself and became convinced he was his own brother John. It wasn't long before measures were taken to depose him and in 1568 his brother, John, did indeed take over the throne. However, Erik's unstable condition continued to cause problems for the new government, with the result that, in 1577, the new king ordered that he be poisoned. It is said that John himself prepared the steaming bowl of arsenic-laced pea soup.

ANNA OF SAXONY

(1544–1577)

nna van Buren was a hunchback who walked with a marked gait. Although unsightly, she was endowed with enormous wealth that attracted no shortage of eligible suitors. She married into royalty to become the wife of William of Orange on August 25, 1561, and her husband was soon to learn that he had taken on far more than her fortune: her unattractive combination of melancholic, aggressive, and suicidal tendencies, an excessive lack of financial restraint, and an incurable propensity towards very public adultery, made her a royal liability of unprecedented scale.

The early years

Anna's childhood had been troubled. By the age of eleven she had lost both her parents and she grew up a lonely and indulged only-child. She came from a long and uneasy line of mentally unstable relatives, and numerous great-grandfathers, uncles, and cousins were said to have suffered from mental illnesses that included severe and suicidal depression and complete mental collapse.

Perhaps not surprisingly, then, Anna's behavior was distinctly unconventional from the earliest days of her marriage. Pregnancy apparently
pushed her over the edge and rendered her vulnerable to increasingly
irrepressible emotional episodes. Political pressures and war in the
Low Countries took William away from home, leaving Anna free to

indulge her excessive boredom by partying wildly and then wallowing in despair, during which times she refused daylight, food, and visitors for days on end. The death of her first child in early infancy, and two further pregnancies in rapid succession within the next two years, no doubt aggravated her nerves. Abandoning all conventions of royal motherhood, she continued to overindulge in alcohol and her mood swings worsened; she neglected her children and grew increasingly aggressive and suicidal.

Filth, slander, and ruination

Events climaxed in 1564, when William decided to remove his elder children from her care. Anna at once withdrew herself from court and turned a deaf ear to her husband's pleas for frugality and respectability. While he was still waging war, she began a very public campaign of her own, accusing him of sexual ineptitude, making an art form of ugly inebriation, and living a life of outrageous and hedonistic excess.

Nevertheless, William continued to write to her, pleading with her to regain some sense of decorum and return to live with him. During this time they met occasionally and she gave birth to two more of his children. But his pleas for a more modest lifestyle were in vain. Always in public, Anna derided his letters and tore them up dismissively.

Surrounded by rigidly respectable nobles, she grew more and more socially isolated. Her aggressive mistreatment of her staff, her very lewd immorality, and her drunken rages did nothing to help her, but it was ultimately her very public affair and subsequent pregnancy with a Flemish man, Jan Rubens, that was to seal her fate.

In 1571 she gave birth to Rubens's daughter, Christina. This was the final insult for William. He refused to recognize Christina as his own child and ensured that Anna would never see her legitimate children again. Her financial situation in disarray, her marriage annulled, and her lover arrested and exiled, Anna never recovered her mental health.

A miserable end

In 1572, she was removed to Beilstein Castle in Germany. The extent of her derangement intensified, so that windows to her rooms had to be bricked up and knives removed from her reach after mealtimes. She grew delusional and talked the talk of a lunatic, all the while foaming at the mouth. Some even mooted the possibility that she was possessed by demons. It was not long before her daughter, Christina, was also permanently removed from her care, to be raised by her father (along with her half-brother, the celebrated painter, Peter Paul Rubens). Anna eventually spiraled out of control and died in this wretched, bricked-up, airless, and darkened cell, five torturous years later. She was thirty-three years old.

RUDOLF II OF AUSTRIA

(1552–1612)

R udolf II was a chronic melancholic whose predilection for the bizarre and curious far outweighed his interests in ruling his country. Although highly intelligent, Rudolf lived in a world of fantasy which eventually led to his undoing.

Spanish influences

Born to a depressive mother who invariably ignored him, and descended from a great-grandmother who deservedly bore the title "Juana la Loca," Rudolf stood every chance of inheriting the family shortcomings. His mother sent him to Madrid in 1564 to complete his education; Rudolf was seriously affected by the cold, grim atmosphere of the Spanish courts and the gloomy monasteries of remote Monseratt. When the young Spanish prince died, and was followed shortly by the Queen, life in Madrid grew ever more oppressive and Rudolf withdrew into his world of make-believe. On his return to Austria in 1571, his parents found him to be a grave young man, prone to aloofness, bad humor, and melancholic mood swings.

Eccentric emperor

Following his crowning as Emperor in 1576, Rudolf's moods grew increasingly dark. The affairs of state crowded his unstable mind, and he swung from excitable involvement to violent frustration. It soon became clear that he was incapable of conducting imperial affairs, and all responsibility was handed over to the chief minister, Wolfgang Rumpf. Relieved of his political duties, Rudolf immersed himself in a world of the strange and wonderful. Soon the royal courts were filled with all manner of eccentrics: from magicians to astronomers (including the highly respected Tycho Brahe and Johannes Kepler) and alchemists to soothsayers. Rudolf spent his nights fixated on the movement of the stars and the planets. He is reported to have amassed a collection of dwarves and exotic beasts, and the corridors of his castle reverberated with the roar of lions and the screeches of strange birds.

Murderous offspring

Rudolf never married despite being betrothed for a number of years to his cousin Isabel. She eventually married Rudolf's younger brother, instead. Rudolf did indulge in an affair with the daughter of the court painter, who bore him a number of peculiar children. One son turned out to be a sadistic murderer who literally tore his lover to pieces and tossed bits of her body around his rooms.

Hallucinations and suicide

As Rudolf grew older, he suffered increasingly from hallucinations and panic attacks. Believing that there was a plot against his life he dismissed his chief minister and holed up in his rooms. Refusing to see anyone, he effectively paralyzed Parliament. Suicide attempts followed: Rudolf tried to slash his throat with a broken pane of glass. Eventually his brother Matthias intervened and forced Rudolf to turn over the monarchy to himself. Rudolf took to drink and died in Prague.

FYODOR I "THE BELLRINGER" OF RUSSIA

(1557–1598)

When Fyodor (sometimes known as Feodor), the son of Ivan the Terrible, reluctantly became the Tsar of Russia in 1584, he was quite happy to let someone else perform all the duties of a ruler. Some believed him a half-wit (including his own father), others a religious visionary.

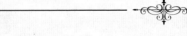

A vote of confidence

Ivan the Terrible's eldest son, Ivan V, was heir to the throne and was tall, tough, and ambitious like his father. But after Ivan the elder killed him in a rage, he was left no choice but to prepare Russia to be ruled by Fyodor, his sole surviving, unwilling, and feeble-minded heir.

Ivan created a council to help his son rule, a virtual public admission that the outgoing Tsar did not believe his son would be a capable incoming Tsar. Ministers on the council fought among themselves, dismaying and bewildering the new Tsar Fyodor I. Their wrangling power-struggle was a mystery to him and his political reluctance was

soon replaced by his complete indifference to affairs of state. Fyodor was more than happy to let his brother-in-law and key advisor, Boris Godunov, become the effectual Tsar.

Disappointed fatherhood

Fyodor had married Irina Godunov before his father's death but their only child to survive pregnancy, a daughter, died in infancy. The good-hearted Fyodor found it too much to bear, and it prompted his mental decline.

The Church and his faith became his only passion. He spent his days deep in ardent prayer. Fyodor's lack of ambition, kindly manner, and religious conviction stood in marked contrast to the terror of his late father. This, coupled with his simple-mindedness and the vacant gaze for which he was noted, was taken by many in Russia at the time to be indicative of his religious inspiration, commanding him a great deal of respect.

Bellringing

The churches and monasteries of the country became a source of endless fascination for Fyodor. As his mental health declined, he developed the habit of traveling the length and breadth of Russia, so that he could ring the bells of as many churches as possible. He loved to hear them peal and call the congregations to worship.

Fyodor died without producing a male heir. This brought about the end of the Rurik dynasty and precipitated the turbulent "Troubled Times" in Russia until the establishment of the Romanov Dynasty in 1613.

Erzsébet Báthory of Hungary

(1560–1614)

E rzsébet Báthory was a Hungarian countess and one of the inspirations for Bram Stoker's *Dracula*. She was the real-life equivalent of a vampire and is reported to have slaughtered six hundred young women so that she could improve her complexion by bathing in and drinking their blood.

The Báthory bloodline

The noble Báthory family was descended from the powerful Hun Gutkeled clan which ruled much of central Europe (modern Poland, Hungary, and Romania) during the first half of the thirteenth century. Fifty years after the death of Erzsébet, the Báthories all but died out. There was much intermarriage and inbreeding within the clan, with inevitable disastrous consequences.

The early years

Erzsébet was a beautiful child with a slender build and a tall frame; she was fit, active, and fluent in four languages. Married off at age fifteen, she found herself the lady of the remote Cachtice castle deep in the Carpathian mountains in what is now central Romania. Her life was dull and provincial and the castle was dark and gloomy. She soon compensated by surrounding herself with lavish amusements and attracting, as lore has it, a retinue of witches, sorcerers, alchemists, and deviant sybarites.

Torture and bloodlust

Her husband, a hardened soldier, was frequently away on military campaigns. Erzsébet had already been introduced to the joys of flagellation by her aunt, and she lost no time in brutally torturing debtors and prisoners from her dungeons to while away her free time.

Bloodbaths and the secret of eternal youth

During her forties, with her looks fading and her husband dead (stabbed by a Bucharest prostitute), Erzsébet's attentions turned to preserving her youth. One day she struck a female servant for a minor indiscretion and drew blood. Observing that the blood seemed to improve her complexion where it had made contact with her own skin, she immediately consulted her alchemists, who concurred, rather than risk a torture session. She resolved henceforth to bathe in and drink the blood of young virgins. She hunted out young peasant women at night and brought them back to the castle where they were hung upside down, alive and naked. Their throats were slit and their bodies drained of blood.

Vampire academy

After five years of abducting virgins of low birth, Erzsébet set up a finishing school in her castle, taking twenty-five girls at a time from good families in the belief that nobler blood would be more beneficial. However, after a sanguinary frenzy, four bodies were thrown over the castle ramparts. The evidence could not be denied, and the Hungarian Emperor Mathias II brought her before a formal hearing in 1610. Being a noblewoman she was immune from execution, so for the remaining four years of her life she was walled up in a tiny chamber in her castle with only a small slot to admit meals. Never once did she utter a word of remorse.

MUSTAFA I OF TURKEY

(1592–1639)

W hen Mustafa I was born, a tradition had been long in place in Turkey that newly enthroned Sultans would execute any contenders to the throne (namely, their brothers). When Mustafa's brother, Ahmed, came to the throne, he decided to spare his brother's life, and instead constructed a windowless prison with a bricked-in entrance for him. This "cage" was to become Mustafa's home from the age of eleven years, until his brother died fourteen years later.

His first period of rule

When Mustafa was first freed from his cage, his mental health was hotly debated by the court. Some insisted he was divinely inspired and a religious visionary. Others saw only his insanity, and interpreted his ranting and raving as psychotic, rather than celestial. His policies and orders did little to gain him anyone's confidence: any kindly page boy or generous farmer would soon find themselves in exalted positions of considerable power and influence at the royal court. This aggravated enough courtiers to tip the balance of public opinion against him. After only three months, Mustafa was returned to his cage.

An incarcerated interregnum

For four years, Mustafa remained locked away with two female slaves. Outside, Osman II, his late brother's thirteen-year-old son, ruled against everything from tobacco and alcohol to his own special forces. At the same time, he worked hard at honing his warrior skills, and practiced with a bow and arrow on living targets around the court. Ultimately, he made himself highly unpopular and was tortured to death in 1622.

By comparison, it would appear that throughout this period Mustafa was relatively content, safe inside his cage. When he was released in 1622, he refused to leave at first, and had to be dragged out at the end of a rope. Mustafa found himself a reluctant Sultan once more.

Bloody revenge in his second reign

Mustafa was again entrusted with governing Turkey. Terrified of this responsibility, and clearly both unhinged and inept, he set out to wreak havoc. He slaughtered all those who had been responsible for pulling him out of the sanctuary of his cage, including his nephew. Farm laborers, donkey drivers, and other unlikely subjects found themselves suddenly promoted to high-ranking positions in his court. He issued a rash of implausible and unreasonable commands. Taxes went unpaid, armed forces went unsalaried, and nationwide anarchy looked more and more likely. Meanwhile Mustafa ran in search of his dead nephew, begging him to return and take over the throne. When next he ordered the execution of Osman's brothers, he was persuaded by his court to renounce the throne, and turn over the monarchy to another of his nephews.

Mustafa was returned to his cage one last time in 1623. He died there sixteen years later.

Istanbul, Turkey

MARIA ELEONORE OF BRANDENBURG

(1599–1655)

Unable to provide her beloved husband, King Gustav II Adolf of Sweden, with a male heir, the attractive, socially accomplished, but inherently unbalanced Queen Maria Eleonore of Brandenburg, lost all sense of reason and succumbed to a hysterical madness which eventually caused her to make repeated attempts on the life of her daughter.

A fruitless marriage

The early months of Maria's marriage seemed pleasant enough. Her husband was a much admired and gracious man with whom she had much in common. The pair shared a great love of music and architecture and spent many hours feasting and being entertained

King Gustav II Adolf of Sweden

by the fashionable dwarves and fools of the court. This honeymoon period was short-lived, however, when during the early months of her first pregnancy, Gustav left to command the siege of Riga and Maria found herself alone and miserable in the dark and gloomy Swedish countryside. Maria eventually miscarried and plunged into despair. Other pregnancies followed, but all ended in miscarriage or stillbirth, contributing to Maria's grief and frustration.

A monster is born

The young queen eventually gave birth to a live baby who was covered in such thick black hair and endowed with such a hugely oversized nose that it was mistaken at first for a boy. Maria was in too fragile a state to be told the truth, so several days passed before anyone would dare to reveal to her that she had in fact given birth to a daughter.

A murderous mother

With her husband the King away at war Maria was left to care for her unwanted child, Christina. Maria subjected her daughter to a number of mysterious "accidents" which included being dropped from a height onto a stone floor, having heavy objects land in her crib, and being inadvertently pushed down the stairs. The baby was eventually given over to the care of King Gustav's half-sister, Katharina.

A grisly end

Unable to cope with the prolonged absences of the King, Maria became more and more unhinged, spending days on end indulging in frenzied weeping and bouts of violent hysteria. When her husband's death on the battlefield was announced, a deranged Maria brought home his embalmed body and, after claiming back her daughter, embarked on an extended orgy of mourning. Maddened by grief, Maria locked herself, her daughter, and the body of the King in dark shrouded rooms where poor Christina was forced to witness the dreadful suffering of her wretched mother and was made to sleep in a bed over which the heart of her dead father swung, encased in a golden casket. By the time of the King's funeral almost a year later, Maria Eleonore had completely lost her mind, and it was not long before she also lost all rights to the pitifully abused Christina who, amazingly, had survived her appalling ordeal.

Murad IV of Turkey

(1612–1640)

Murad IV became Sultan of Turkey at the age of eleven. He was a misogynist, an alcoholic, and a homicidal maniac. Ruthlessly aggressive, excessively intolerant, and feared by all, his seventeen-year reign was a bloodbath on a colossal scale.

Early years

Murad's uncle (Mustafa I) and brother (Osman II) were insane. His mother was power-hungry and at first governed her son (and Turkey) from the harem. So extreme were her aspirations to assert herself that she even attempted to entice him into homosexuality, presenting him with attractive young boys to enjoy, rather than the girls of the harem, whose bickering and wrangling she tired of and whose influence she mistrusted.

As a result of her overbearing and domineering mothering, Murad developed a lifelong misogyny. In his brief adulthood, he enjoyed using women for live target practice; ordered his canons to fire at a boat full of women simply because they were there; and drowned another group of women whose singing he had taken a dislike to. He was merciless towards his harem, and subjected them to humiliations while guarding them so jealously that he did not hesitate to execute anyone he suspected of desiring them.

Killing spree

Early in Murad's reign, the Turkish cavalry were undisciplined and they humiliated him by revolting. Murad asserted his authority over his troops and his court with such brutality that more than twenty thousand people died.

He developed a seemingly insatiable passion for assassination and execution. He would pass an evening wandering the streets accompanied by his executioner and a variety of tools and weapons, looking for miscreants to execute. He was particularly fond of personally decapitating men with thick necks. He would spike, shoot, or behead his servants and staff for trivial reasons. In the last years of his life, he regularly careened through the streets at night, drunk and half-naked, sword held aloft, running through anyone he passed by. It is estimated that at least twenty-five thousand people perished as a result of Murad's killing sprees.

Paranoia

The paranoia and jealousy that characterized Murad's brutal rule extended to his policies. He prohibited the consumption of alcohol, tobacco, and coffee on the basis that, wherever people gathered publicly to partake, they could also indulge in unfavorable discussions about their Sultan. While anyone caught drinking or smoking was mercilessly executed, Murad enjoyed all three to excess, and is believed to have died from cirrhosis of the liver, exacerbated by a fit of terror he suffered while witnessing an eclipse.

Murad's own family was not spared his murdering frenzy: he killed all but one of his own brothers, in one case because he had been humiliated in a jousting contest which his brother, Beyazid, had won. The only brother whose life he spared was Ibrahim, whom he deemed too deranged to present a threat. Even then, in his dying days, Murad ordered his brother's death. It was only the intervention of their mother that spared Ibrahim's life.

IBRAHIM I OF TURKEY

(1615–1648)

I brahim I of Turkey was a murderously violent and cold-hearted man whose domestic pleasures included mass rape and the attempted murder of his own son.

Bizarre beginnings

From infancy, Ibrahim had been locked up and isolated in the "Cage," a prison chamber where sultans sequestered potential rivals to their throne. The only sibling kept alive by his brother the Sultan Murad IV, Ibrahim lived in constant dread, ignorant as to whether or not each new dawn would be his last. But the fates smiled upon Ibrahim, and in 1640, following the death of Murad IV, he was declared the new Sultan. Unwilling at first to leave his prison, and believing the news to be a gruesome practical joke, Ibrahim was only convinced of his good fortune when Murad's corpse was delivered to the doors of his prison.

Grand-scale debauchery

Ibrahim took to his new role of Sultan with terrifying relish. He ran amok, raping women and increasing the size of his harem to formidable proportions. His fetishes bordered on the perverse, and his favorites in the harem were often chosen by their ability to satisfy them.

Blood thirsty father

The inevitable consequence of Ibrahim's profligacy was offspring, all of whom he treated with the same callous disregard he showed their mothers. He threw his firstborn son into a pool of water, and although the child survived, Ibrahim later thrust a dagger through his forehead for joking around at an inopportune moment.

Jealous revenge

When Ibrahim heard that a member of his harem had been unfaithful to him, he exacted his revenge on a colossal scale. He tortured all 280 terrified women, and when they refused to divulge the guilty party's name he had them bundled into weighted sacks and thrown into the river Bosporus.

Vulgar excess

Ibrahim had expensive tastes. He raided businesses throughout the Empire to satisfy his desire for jewels, perfumes, and exotic goods, and he insisted on performing his sexual conquests on beds of sable and draping his clothes and walls with every available fur. The country sank into chaos while Ibrahim carried on his murderous orgy of excess. Revolt was not long in coming, and in 1648 Ibrahim was deposed and thrown back into his cage. Within a week, court-appointed executioners strangled him to death.

CHRISTINA OF SWEDEN

(1626–1689)

C hristina was an intelligent, capable monarch who loved to shock and flout all convention. She was headstrong, extroverted, and narcissistic. Confused sexuality likely contributed to her erratic reign.

An ambiguous start

When King Gustavus Adolphus (Gustav Adolph II) and his wife Queen Maria discovered they were expecting a child, they were convinced it would be a boy. They even consulted with wise women and soothsayers, who assured them they would have their male heir. And when the baby was first delivered, it was covered in hair and reportedly cried with a deep voice so distinctively male that at first Gustavus was told he had his son. There appears to have been some ambiguity about the child's gender because the midwives only decided later that the baby was in fact a girl.

Undeterred, the King determined that his daughter should be raised as a Prince. Consequently, Christina was educated in Latin and five other

European languages, the sciences and arts, and philosophy. She was also trained in the disciplines of swordsmanship and horsemanship. She frequently dressed as a man.

While her father idolized her, her mother failed to bond with Christina at birth, and thereafter would have very little to do with her. There were many rumors as to the reason for this rejection, but the most valid seemed to be Maria's envy: she was a vacuous woman, and was said to be wildly jealous of her husband's devotion to Christina. On several occasions, freak "accidents" almost killed the young princess. She was frequently dropped on the floor as an infant and narrowly avoided being hit by falling beams and items of heavy furniture. Her "accident-prone" childhood resulted in one of Christina's shoulders being permanently higher than the other, adding physical deformity to her already idiosyncratic persona.

Capable queen

When Christina was just six years old, her beloved father was killed on the battlefield. As heiress presumptive, she ruled with the assistance of a council until she was eighteen, and thereafter was crowned Queen in her own right. At first, she proved a capable monarch, if highly autonomous and disinclined to follow the advice of her council. As she matured, her headstrong self-reliance became more pronounced. Pressured by her court to marry, and criticized for her profligate spending on the increasing ranks of her nobles, Christina abdicated her throne in 1654, claiming her desire to become a Catholic.

After she was no longer Queen of Sweden, she attempted to have herself instated first as Queen of Naples, and then of Poland. Both plans failed. She once had an ex-lover executed at midnight in her apartments in Versailles, Paris, having first accused him of treason, because he had divulged her secrets to Oliver Cromwell of England.

Flouting convention

Christina was never one for following convention and her life was marked by contradictions. She had no interest in her appearance: she rarely combed her hair and gave little thought to her clothing. She pursued a life of shameless licentiousness, and yet converted to Catholicism, although it was an illegal religion in Sweden. Despite much pressure from her council, she resolutely refused to marry. She was linked romantically to several individuals, male and female, but was said to have died a virgin. She often donned a man's wig and clothing. When she left Sweden following her abdication, she dressed as a man and traveled incognito across Europe. Her masculine physique and attributes drew attention wherever she went: she would sit watching a musical or theatrical performance, swearing like a soldier, and swinging her legs over the arms of her chair. In Rome she indulged in a passionate (yet allegedly platonic) affair with a cardinal, and argued with Popes. She was famous for her intelligent queenship, and yet gave up her throne. Her final years were spent in Rome and Spain. She was buried in St. Peter's Basilica.

LOUIS XIV OF FRANCE

(1638–1715)

L ouis XIV of France has gone down in history as one of the most remarkable monarchs of all time, not least because of his astonishing reign of seventy-two years, during which France became one of the strongest powers in Europe. He was also renowned for an insatiable sexual appetite that increased the size of his family and, by extension, the monarchy.

Early days

Louis was the long awaited child of Louis XIII and Anne of Austria, born to them after twenty-three years of marriage. He became King at age four, although the early years of his reign were controlled by the chief minister, Cardinal Mazarin.

His wives

Louis was short in stature but made up for what he lacked in height by tottering around in high heels and wearing outlandish wigs of towering

proportions. Although disinclined to bathe more than twice a year, he never wanted for female conquests.

Unable to marry his first love for political reasons, Louis was forced into marriage with the lumpish and obese Maria-Thérèse of Austria. Louis managed to overcome his physical loathing of his wife and spent at least part of every night in her bed. The poor woman found herself a mere baby-making machine. After suffering from seven pregnancies and an over-strained heart, she was killed by zealous court physicians, who accidentally bled her to death.

Louis married his second wife, the plain and practical Madame de Maintenon, in secret. Madame de Maintenon learned to refuse Louis's sexual demands on occasion, which kept him interested in her for the entirety of their marriage. In fact, on reaching the age of seventy-five, Madame was heard to complain that the twice daily demands of her seventy-year-old husband were becoming rather tiring.

His mistresses

Louis was in the habit of keeping at least four mistresses on the go at any one time. He was not in the least bit choosy, and many a servant girl had to avoid getting too close, lest she be whisked off to his bed-chamber. Any passing female would do. Louis fathered a vast amount of illegitimate children, all of whom put a severe strain on the French economy, and all of whom he allowed to marry into the royal family and thereby dilute the bloodline.

Age-old exploits

Louis had already contracted gonorrhea at the age of seventeen, so it was no surprise that later on in life he should suffer from syphilis. Not that the disease slowed him down in any sense; on the contrary, his sexual exploits became his only pleasure in life, and it was a gangrenous leg which finally killed him aged seventy-six.

Maria-Therese

CHARLES II OF SPAIN

(1661–1700)

C harles II was the unfortunate product of years of incestuous intermarriages and massive inbreeding that likely endowed him with inherited physical disorders and almost certainly saddled him with a case of congenital syphilis. Although hideously disfigured and feeble of mind, his birth was greeted with elation by the Spanish people, who had feared a disputed succession if his father Philip IV left no heir. Subsequently, the monstrous child became known as "The Desired" or, more fittingly, "The Bewitched."

A royal monstrosity

Born with a massively misshapen head, a grotesquely jutting jaw, and a tongue so thick it prevented normal speech, Charles II was a far cry from your usual monarch when he ascended to the throne of Spain at the age of three. Fed exclusively on the milk of wet nurses until the age of six, Charles was overprotected and mollycoddled. He was discouraged from walking until adulthood, and his already feeble mind was left to rot in a perpetual infancy. Such was the extent of his enforced inertia

that the lumpish King was not even expected to wash. He understood neither politics nor etiquette, and he only left his rooms on occasion to indulge in a spot of shooting; the only time he ever exhibited any form of traditionally masculine behavior.

A failure in the royal bedchamber

At eighteen, Charles was married to the dim but willing Marie Louise of Orleans. The trials within the marital bedchamber were myriad, with the childlike King unable to perform his royal duties to any degree of competency. Despondent in her issueless marriage, Marie Louise sought refuge in gluttony and reportedly gorged herself to an agonizing death at age twenty-seven. The King, whose advisors were still desperate for a royal heir, was soon married to Maria Anna of Pfalz-Neuburg. Despite being exorcised to increase her fertility, she too failed to produce an heir.

The final decline

The King's health deteriorated rapidly, and he spent his latter years a bald, toothless, dribbling wreck, prone to lameness, weeping ulcers, diseased bones, and fits. During his last days he called for the bodies of his dead relatives and first wife to be exhumed from their graves so he could gaze upon their rotted faces one last time. A series of powerful fits ended his life at the age of thirty-eight.

Ivan "The Ignorant" of Russia

(1666–1696)

I van V of Russia was a quiet, timid, and unassuming man. Learning-disabled, physically challenged, and only partially sighted, he was manipulated by his family and his political faction in his early years, and by his sister in his later years. He held the throne but never exerted any power and was known as Ivan the Ignorant.

Early years

Ivan was one of thirteen children born to Tsar Alexis I and his first wife, Tsarina Maria Miloslawskaya. All were sickly children: most died either in infancy or early childhood. Ivan was nervous and dependent, with stammered speech, poor sight, and multiple other disabilities. He was never groomed for the throne. His

mother died when he was only three years old, whereupon his father remarried and sired a healthy son, Peter.

Upon the Tsar Alexis's death, the families of the two Tsarina's fought for power. Ivan was suddenly thrust into the political limelight, a position for which he had not been prepared and was ill-equipped. In the uncertainty of the times, an uprising by an angry Moscow mob took place, and during the struggle Ivan witnessed the slaughter of many relatives as irate Muscovites scoured the palace.

Political pawn

Political supporters who wanted Ivan's maternal lineage to remain in power insisted that he and his half-brother, Peter, rule as co-Tsars. The young Peter was more than up for the job; Ivan meanwhile sat vacant and disaffected, staring at the floor and taking in little of what was going on around him. He was brought out for public ceremonies (walking only with the help of others), and kept his supporters happy with his nominal role, but in practice he did nothing and understood little.

His sister, Sophia (an able and ambitious woman who ran Russia while her brother and half-brother were still too young to govern independently), determined to find her challenged sibling a wife. In the ordinary course of things this would have presented many difficulties: Ivan was not the strong, dashing, and able figure his half-brother Peter presented.

Nevertheless, despite his disabilities, he was a Tsar and many Russian aristocrats were excited by the prospect of marrying royalty. The chance of netting a gentle Tsar, who spent his days in quiet contemplation and prayer, rather than an aggressive tyrant, was even more attractive.

After an initial period of anticipation, Ivan and his wife, the beautiful and self-possessed Praskovia, gave birth to five daughters, of which three survived.

Early death

Ivan withdrew completely from affairs of state, and as his twenties progressed he rarely appeared in public. He spent his days with his wife and devoted hours to fasting and prayer, often forgoing sleep to stay up and pray through the night. His paralysis grew more pervasive and his impaired sight gave way to blindness. The learning difficulties of his childhood turned to early-onset senility and he died at the age of twenty-nine, leaving his brother, Peter the Great, free to rule Russia alone.

GIAN GASTONE DE' MEDICI

(1671–1737)

G ian Gastone was a wretched, depressive drunk, who over-compensated for his despondent self-indulgence with drunken orgies, vast numbers of male prostitutes, and other outrageous conduct. Unfortunately for the Medici dynasty, for whom he was to be the last remaining male and the last grand duke, he was repulsed by his wife and never sired children. In the end, he lost his grip on reality as well as morality, and refused even to get out of bed.

Oppressive childhood

Gian Gastone's parents were a spectacularly ill-matched couple whose mutual loathing drove them to put several hundred miles between themselves. In fact his mother, Marguerite Louise of France, was so repulsed by her husband that she tried to miscarry all his children, including Gian Gastone. When that proved unsuccessful, she went out of her way to avoid them all. Not surprisingly, Gastone grew to be a solitary child, given to bouts of depression from a very early age.

Wretched marriage

Gastone's likely homosexuality was a source of contention to his religiously fervent father, Cosimo III. To make matters worse, Cosimo was acutely aware that his son needed an heir so, dismissing his sexual proclivities, he married him off to a wealthy but arrogant and exceptionally unattractive German widow, Anne Marie Francesca. The couple soon learned to loathe each other and Gastone's depression worsened. Anne Marie's immense size and obsessive love of horses drove him to gambling and drinking on a colossal scale.

A pimp, by royal appointment

Gastone left his wife and moved to Prague where he began a love affair with a man named Giuliano Dami, who also organized a readily available selection of young men and women, for the pleasure of whose company Gastone was always willing to pay. Gastone's whoring grew to the point of obsession: by the early eighteenth century, back in Florence, he gained a reputation for public displays of a distinctly un-regal behavior, frequently leaving functions blind drunk and soaked in his own urine and vomit. His tastes became more depraved than ever: reports suggest he developed a liking for sadomasochistic sexual encounters, especially with brawny men, who often left him injured.

Bed-ridden

By the latter years of his life, sex, alcohol, and gambling were no longer enough to stave off the worst effects of his depression. His personal grooming suffered: the urine and vomit was simply wiped away with his wig, and his hair and nails were left to grow. By 1730, the fifty-nine-year-old took up permanent residence in his bed. He surrounded himself with his servants and whores, moved his dogs in with him, and even conducted his affairs of state from his bed. He stayed there for the last six years of his life. The bed itself grew ever filthier, filled with the putrid debris of his self-destruction. For a brief while, his brother's widow had periodically organized the cleaning of the royal bed, but when she died in 1731, no one was brave enough to take on the job and the bed was left to rot. Gastone died lame, blind, and senile.

PETER THE GREAT OF RUSSIA

 (1672–1725)

P eter the Great was a merciless and despotic Tsar of Russia. He was plagued by paranoia and brutal to the point of sadistic psychosis. He was also a chronic alcoholic, and appears to have been so addicted to sex that he considered it a royal duty to impregnate vast numbers of women.

The early years

When his older half-brother died in 1682, Peter was still only ten years old and had a rival claim to the throne with his learning-disabled half-brother, Ivan. In the inevitable struggle for power that followed, Peter was forced to witness the slaughter of many of his friends and relations. During the massacre, Peter was eyewitness to the grisly murder of an uncle, torn apart at the hands of an incensed mob. The trauma of these experiences may have desensitized the young Peter and could account for the ferocious assassinations for which he was notorious in adulthood.

Power and paranoia

As Tsar, Peter displayed a lethal combination of a raging fear of betrayal and a love of violent reprisal.

When his half sister, Sophia, attempted a coup in 1698, it was quickly quashed. He ordered a mass-execution of all the rebels, beheading several and hanging hundreds more all over Moscow. He took the further precaution of hanging a selection of corpses outside the convent window to which Sophia had been banished. She reportedly went mad as a result.

Peter was impressed by all things European, particularly after completing his two-year Grand Tour in 1698, despite leaving a trail of destruction behind him in every country house and palace where he stayed. Among his many reforms aimed at modernizing Russia was his bizarre insistence that his courtiers shave off their long, orthodox beards; any who wished to retain their beard would be heavily taxed for the privilege.

His reforms were universally unpopular, but any opposition was brutally silenced with public floggings, mutilations, and executions. None of his countrymen were spared. When his own son, Alexei, spoke out in criticism of his father, then left Russia altogether in 1716, Peter became convinced he was planning a coup and had him arrested, imprisoned, tortured, and tried for treason. Peter conducted some of the interrogations himself. Ultimately condemned to death, Alexei died before his execution, as a result of the horrific injuries sustained under torture.

Sexually voracious

In his personal life, Peter prided himself upon his sexual prowess. He was a striking figure, standing six-feet five-inches tall, with deep green eyes. During both of his marriages, his wives' ladies-in-waiting were fair game, and it is reported that of the four hundred or so in the royal employ at any one time, one in four had been conquests. At social functions, Peter would whisk away any young lady who caught his eye, and seduce women without so much as closing the door to prevent their husbands from watching. When one such assignation led to him contracting syphilis, he was furious and ordered the woman's husband to give the lady in question a sound whipping as punishment.

Pickled heads

From his wives and mistresses, by contrast, Peter demanded complete loyalty. One mistress of long standing, Mary Hamilton, was beheaded for her infidelity. As her head fell into the basket below, he picked it up, kissed it, and let it fall back into the dirt. Fifty years later, Catherine the Great found Mary's head, preserved in alcohol, in the Royal Gallery.

A similar fate befell William Mons, with whom Tsarina Catherine, Peter's second wife, had an indiscreet affair. The Tsar was enraged and ordered her to take a front seat at his execution. That night, and for several thereafter, she found herself sleeping alongside the pickled head of her late lover. She never admitted her affair to her husband, who eventually relented. But Mons's head was also found in a jar, next to that of Mary Hamilton.

Catherine I, wife of Peter the Great

PHILIP V OF SPAIN

(1683–1746)

P hilip V was a cold, dull man with both a voracious sexual appetite and an over-zealous religious streak, the tension between which likely aggravated his unbalanced mind.

A man of two halves

Philip's life was governed by two primary concerns: an unswerving devotion to the Catholic faith, and an unhealthy addiction to vast quantities of sex. As his obsessions were so obviously at odds with one another, he spent most of his time in a state of abject guilt; unburdening himself in the confessional box one minute, then finding himself at the whim of his carnal urges the next. His strong faith forbade his taking mistresses, so it was down to his two wives to cope with the full force of his rampant demands. His first wife, who was only fourteen when they married, had a very tough time of it, and the toll of sleepless nights and four pregnancies soon took her to the grave. It is said that Philip had to be pulled off her dying body as he attempted to enjoy her charms one last time.

Hysteria and madness

The sex-starved King did not wait long before taking himself a second wife. But Elisabeth Farnese of Parma withheld her sexual services, reducing Philip to a gibbering wreck until she found herself not only master of the King, but effective ruler of Spain to boot. Relieved of all kingly pressures, Philip suffered his first major mental breakdown and locked himself in his chambers, refusing to see anyone except the Queen, and only then if she was willing to sleep with him. Delusional and half-mad, the King shuffled through the courts bent and crumpled, looking twice his age.

Reluctant ruler

Philip sank in and out of madness. In one rare lucid moment he astonished everyone by announcing his abdication in favor of his son, Louis I. He had recognized his own inabilities and wished to retreat into a quiet life of solitude. Much to his horror, however, Louis I died of smallpox seven months later, and Philip was forced to take to the throne once more.

A dismal ending

The burden of royal responsibilities took its toll on Philip and he descended into a manic depression which saw him regularly howling and screaming, and violently attacking all those around him. He hobbled around in stinking rags, his hair long and unkempt. He refused to bathe, shave, or cut his fingernails and toenails. He suffered from extreme lethargy and was convinced he could not walk because one foot was too large and the other too small. He bit chunks of flesh from his own body, then laughed hysterically or sang for hours. He was kept well out of sight and before long sank into an extended vacant trance which ended in a fatal stroke as he lay in a bed of his own filth.

FREDERICK WILLIAM I OF PRUSSIA

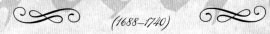

(1688–1740)

Frederick William I of Prussia, although remembered as a superb administrator who transformed his country into a wealthy and enlightened state was, behind closed doors, a manic bully and a miser of epic proportions. He harbored an unerring passion for the military life, and reveled in forcing his family to live a regimented, frugal, and disciplined existence.

The early years

Frederick William grew up in the comfortable and lavish surroundings of his father's court. A man of expensive tastes, Frederick's father was inspired by the opulence of the French royalty, and plunged his country into debt in order to finance his extravagant lifestyle. Frederick was sickened by this frivolous mismanagement and vowed to run things differently when it was his turn to rule.

The Prussian Scrooge

When Frederick took to the throne in 1713, he immediately slashed royal expenditures to the bare minimum. So many servants were sacked that the Royal Family had to help themselves to their own meals and wash up afterwards. Every penny spent, every egg eaten, and every candle burned had to be accounted for. The King was parsimonious in the extreme, and is reported to have marched through the streets ripping excessive and flamboyant trimmings from the dresses of every passing woman.

A military obsession

From boyhood Frederick had indulged his passion for all things military, but as King he allowed his preoccupation to soar, creating an incredible regiment which consisted of only very tall soldiers. These giants were recruited from all over Europe, with Frederick sending out, agents to pay families for handing over their tallest sons. If they didn't Frederick's agents would simply kidnap them. Frederick was devoted to his "Potsdam Giants," and never once risked them in battle, preferring instead to have them sit for portraits, or march them through his bedroom when he was feeling under the weather. When the kidnappings grew excessive and unacceptable (a very lofty priest was once abducted mid-sermon), Frederick began a breeding program, matching his soldiers to equally towering women. It proved an unsatisfactory and very slow procedure for sustaining the army.

Violent parenting

Frederick proved to be a violent and tyrannical father. His eldest son, Fritz, who bore the brunt of his rages, failed to grow into Frederick's ideal of a fine young solider. He was awakened each morning by the blast of cannon fire and by the age of six was put in charge of his own regiment. He was beaten harshly for falling off his horse and for daring to wear gloves in freezing weather. He was regularly the victim of frenzied attacks, suffering many public and bloody beatings at his father's hands. When the young Fritz decided enough was enough and tried to flee the country, Frederick had him captured and forced him to witness the brutal execution of his best friend.

An undignified ending

Frederick grew viler with every passing year, succumbing to blind rages and striking out viciously at anyone who crossed his path. He became grotesquely swollen, and tormented by agonizing pains, dropsy, gout, and insomnia that reduced him to endlessly hobbling along the corridors at night and weeping incessantly throughout the day. He died bloated and in pain.

ANNA I OF RUSSIA

(1693–1740)

This cruel and dispassionate woman spread alarm and terror throughout her reign; she spoke like a man, dressed like a man, and delighted in sinister practical jokes and ritual humiliations.

Dysfunctional family

Anna was the niece of Peter the Great and the daughter of Ivan V and Czarina Praskovia. Her closest family all showed signs of mental aberration, and growing up in what must have seemed like a lunatic asylum—surrounded by her mother's coterie of dwarves, jesters, and simpletons—Anna understandably developed a skewed view of the world.

A short-lived marriage

When she was seventeen, Anna was married to the dashing Duke of Courland. Their wedding was a never-ending spectacle of excess and extravagance, which it seemed the poor duke could not cope with. He died of over-indulgence a mere six weeks later.

The house of ice

Anna was unexpectedly made Empress in 1730. It was hoped she would agree to be nothing more than a figurehead who allowed the powerful nobles to rule in her name. It was not to be: Anna took immediate control (with the help of her Imperial guards) and began a campaign of noble intimidation. She famously arranged for one prince, Michael Golitsyn (an aristocrat who annoyed her), to be wed to an ugly old crone. She had them both dressed as clowns and paraded through the streets with an entourage of farmyard animals. After the official ceremony the humiliated pair was stripped naked and ensconced in a specially constructed palace of ice, where they were made to lie all night on a frozen bed.

Joker empress

Anna loved nothing more than to play practical jokes—the sicker and more degrading the better. She used her powers to intimidate and humiliate not only her subjects, but her confidantes at court. During her reign, she used Russia's wealth to surround herself in luxuries while the people of her country starved. Those who dared protest had their tongues ripped out or were exiled to the wastelands of Siberia. She found it amusing to hang her cooks for singeing food and thought nothing of ordering overweight noblewomen to be stuffed with pies until they passed out. Many a high-ranking official found himself appointed keeper of one of her dogs, and many were ordered to play the role of jester, or to spend hours consigned to a corner where they were forced to impersonate chickens.

Promiscuous romps

Anna never remarried, preferring instead to romp through her courts

sleeping with whomever she fancied, whatever their social status or sex. She was unashamed of her actions and would openly conduct her official business while in bed caressing a young servant girl. She is said to have turned one of her palaces into a brothel and instructed her officials to scour the country for tall, good-looking girls with which to amuse herself. Anna died of kidney disease at age forty-seven.

BARBARA OF PORTUGAL

(1711–1758)

Princess Barbara of Portugal was a corpulent asthmatic with a major neurosis that succeeded in earning her the contempt of all Spain, where she ruled as Queen upon the death of her father-in-law, King Philip V of Spain.

Promising childhood

Unlike the typical raving royal, Princess Barbara had a happy childhood, received a fine education, and was a highly talented harpsichord player. She was so adept at music that her tutor, the famous composer Scarlatti, moved with her to Madrid when she married the heir to the Spanish throne. She composed a staggering five hundred and fifty-five sonatas for harpsichord.

Happy marriage

Barbara was no beauty, and her vast size was said to have been so shocking that, upon the occasion of their first meeting, her royal fiancé, Prince Ferdinand of Spain, recoiled in horror.

However, against all odds, their shared love of music did help foster something of a harmonious marriage. The only area of contention was that her husband had a sexually voracious appetite. Very soon, Barbara learned to manipulate her husband's sexual needs, conniving to gain the upper hand, so that Ferdinand was often at her mercy.

Despite their considerable efforts, they did not have children.

Neurosis

Ferdinand's obsessive fear of assassination seems to have been taken up by Barbara, so that she developed a complex all of her own. Convinced that she would face early widowhood, and, worse, would suffer it in a foreign country, she became overwhelmed by a fear of living out her dotage in poverty. In reaction, she began to display an extreme and very public attachment to money, from the earliest days of her husband's accession to the throne. To the annoyance of the Spanish court and the people beyond, she scrimped, saved, and hoarded wherever she could, making a neurosis out of her parsimony.

Gruesome death

In 1757, a strange illness left Barbara covered in boils. The illness was slow, lingering, and excruciatingly painful. She was confined to bed where she remained for another eleven months. Her asthma, which had plagued her all her life, had also become debilitating, and her once immense body withered away, so that by her death at age forty-six, she was wan, gaunt, and skeletal.

A bizarre legacy

Upon her death, her apartment was found to be filled to the ceiling with money, all of it Spanish, amounting to a fortune far in excess of anything she could have hoped to have needed to see her through even the longest widowhood.

Barbara bequeathed her entire fortune to her brother, Joseph I of Portugal. Except for the convent she had built, to which she had planned to retreat upon the death of her husband, she had seen to it that Spain would not benefit from any of the money she had hoarded at its expense. Her husband outlived her by nearly a year.

FERDINAND VI OF SPAIN

(1713–1759)

Ferdinand VI was the only son of Philip V by his first wife, Maria Luisa of Savoy. A fickle and indolent man who suffered from acute paranoia, sex addiction, and uncontrollable rages, Ferdinand eventually became suicidal and succumbed to total insanity.

Seeds of self-doubt

Ferdinand's early years were depressive. Having lost his own mother he had to suffer the abusive attentions of his father's second wife, Elizabeth Farnese. This highly unpleasant woman made it abundantly clear that she had feelings only for her own children. She treated Ferdinand with a mixture of disdain and loathing, and frequently pit him against her own son. Ferdinand grew to maturity with an intense self-hatred and low self-esteem.

Sex slave

At the age of fifteen, Ferdinand married the distinctly plain and corpulent Barbara of Portugal. He is said to have winced in horror when he first set eyes on her. Much to everyone's surprise however, there was something in the pockmarked visage and neurotic personality of his new wife that was to prove deeply attractive to Ferdinand. He lived completely under her spell, doing anything that was required in order to spend an extra hour holed up together with her in the royal bedchamber.

An incompetent king

When Ferdinand ascended to the throne in 1746, it was clear he was not up to the job. Crippled by shyness and a total lack of self-worth, he was unable to make the smallest of decisions. It was left to his domineering wife to control public affairs and to influence his actions. Plagued by the constant dread of assassination attempts, Ferdinand grew ever more depressed and escaped into the world of opera, becoming unnaturally fixated with the famous singer Farinelli. He would have the virtuoso installed on a boat and would sail down the river Taag with Farinelli singing at the top of his voice.

A crazed ending

The death of his adored wife broke Ferdinand's heart and mind. Crazed with grief, Ferdinand finally lost his tenuous grip on reality. He plunged into a black hole of despair, and raged about the courts dressed

only in his nightshirt, randomly attacking servants and ranting wildly at the world. He refused to eat and starved himself until skeletal, then binged himself back to obesity. He spent days on his feet refusing to sit or lie down, as he was convinced that if he did so he would surely die. He refused to wash, dress, or see anyone and his fits of rage grew ever more violent and self-destructive. He attempted to take his own life by strangling himself with napkins, hanging himself with sheets, stabbing himself with scissors, and begging his doctors to poison him and end his misery. When all this failed, he spent hours banging his head against walls. After one such episode, he fell into a state of utter prostration and finally died of natural causes at the age of forty-five.

CATHERINE THE GREAT OF RUSSIA

(1729–1796)

C atherine the Great was not only an enlightened ruler, cred-
ited with establishing the Russian Empire as a great power,
she was also a formidable woman, cursed with a monumen-
tal libido. Her sexual excesses became the stuff of legend.

Early betrothal

Born a German princess in the Prussian city of Stettin, Catherine was
informed at an early age that she was to marry the heir to the Russian
throne, Grand Duke Peter. This stunted and feeble-minded young man
proved so repulsive in appearance that Catherine spent weeks living
in dread of her wedding night. As luck would have it, the wedding
was postponed while Peter battled smallpox and turned increasingly
to alcohol which, not surprisingly, added nothing to his already dull
charms. So it was that when her wedding day eventually arrived, Catherine found herself marrying an odious creature, made more nauseating
by his recently acquired baldness and pockmarked skin.

A rude awakening

It wasn't long before the question of an heir raised its ugly head and Peter, who suffered a physical malformation of his sexual organs, underwent an operation to correct the problem. The procedure was a complete success and Peter eventually did his duty by his wife. Unbeknownst to him however, Catherine was already pregnant by her first lover, the nobleman Serge Saltykov, and had developed an insatiable appetite for carnal sport which was to last her a life time.

An army of lovers

Catherine began on an epic sex-fest, dragging officers and politicians to her bed with breathtaking abandon. She hid her many pregnancies under the wide-skirted dresses of the time and would have the babies whisked away the moment they were born. She treated her lovers generously and when she tired of them would promote them to a higher rank or present them with a costly gift. One of her lovers, Prince Grigori Potemkin, a cavalry officer, remained at court when their affair ended and took to searching out young, virile men to satisfy the randy empress. He would pick only the most handsome and would test the quality of their performances on the ladies-in-waiting before ushering them to Catherine's chambers.

Tiring of her husband's inadequacies between the sheets and his lack of authority as ruler, Catherine had him murdered by an abandoned lover and grabbed the throne for herself. She was to prove a far more capable monarch than her hapless husband would ever have been.

Horseplay

Catherine suffered a stroke at age sixty-seven and died the following evening. Her sexual exploits were so notorious, however, that one legend of her demise continues to upstage the truth: It is reputed that, unable to find any man adequately equipped to satisfy her, Catherine attempted intimate relations with a horse, and died when the confused creature lost its balance and crushed her to death.

MARIA I OF PORTUGAL

(1734–1816)

Maria Francisca, who was to become Maria I of Portugal, was the product of two bloodlines tainted with traces of madness. Grandfathers on both of her father's and mother's sides were notorious for their religious mania and sexual promiscuity, so it comes as no surprise that Maria eventually fell victim to her family's peculiarities.

Incestuous marriage

She married her older uncle Pedro, her father's younger brother, when she was twenty-five. By all accounts it was a very happy marriage, and the two spent many hours attending various church ceremonies and several masses each day. The devoted Pedro built her a pink palace where they lived a pious life with their three surviving children.

Early days as Queen

Maria's father was a lackadaisical King who left all decisions to his trusted minister, the Marquis of Pombal. The Marquis believed that

Queen Maria I and King Pedro III

Portugal's strong Catholic foundations were a hindrance to the nation's progress, so during his rule terror reigned over the country with many religious men persecuted and left to rot in prison for daring to question him. On her ascension to the throne following her father's death, Maria attempted to undo some of the harm wrought by dismissing Pombal and releasing all of his prisoners. Maria feared that her father would be damned to hell for allowing Pombal to persecute so many men of God. This fear began to overwhelm her senses as she slid deliriously into religious mania.

The madness takes over

When her beloved Pedro died in 1786, Maria withdrew into a prayer-filled grief. The subsequent deaths of her eldest son and only surviving daughter unhinged her mind even further and plunged her into a deep and dreadful psychosis. Convinced of her sure passage to hell to join her misguided father, the Queen began to indulge in gluttony and language of a lewd nature. She claimed that she regularly saw her father's blackened and tortured image being dragged into a crowd of hideous demons.

Barmy in Brazil

The Bible-banging queen was eventually declared mad and confined to her chambers, where she lay all day in darkness, gnashing her teeth. Her slightly saner, snuff-addicted son, Joao, was named Prince Regent in 1799, and together with his wife, Carlota, took over all royal duties. When Napoleon invaded Portugal in 1807 the royals fled to Brazil and were warmly welcomed by the natives of Rio de Janerio. Maria, however, was convinced she had entered the fires of hell for good when she witnessed the native's ceremonial welcoming dance. She was carted off to an old and secluded convent where she spent the rest of her days believing she was being pursued by the Devil himself.

GEORGE III OF ENGLAND

(1738–1820)

George III was a troubled king who ruled England from 1760. During his lucid periods he was a likeable monarch, a loyal husband, and a fond, if authoritarian, father. But he suffered a crippling mental degeneration, with bouts of severe instability, before a lingering ten-year episode which lasted until his merciful death at the age of eighty-one.

Early mental health

George was a sullen, challenging child, given to melancholy and rage. Though his desire for learning was evident well into adulthood, he was never a gifted student, hindered by sluggishness and always hopelessly unfocused.

In the early years of his monarchy, he was highly dependent upon dubious advisors. Twice he came close to abdication. His private life was no less tumultuous: from the age of twenty-one, he began a long and unrequited infatuation with fifteen-year-old Sarah Lennox, daughter

of the Duke of Richmond. But he took his responsibility seriously, agonizing over his selection of a wife. He married Sophia Charlotte of Mecklenburg-Strelitz, and with her sired fifteen children.

Barbarous quackery

When the first episode of George's madness took hold in 1788, it was catastrophic. His close friends watched aghast as he lay foaming at the mouth, doubled up with violent stomach cramps, delirious and fighting for breath. In a bizarre display of loyalty, his courtiers took to feigning insanity in sympathy, apparently keen to lessen the impact of the King's.

His condition spiraled out of control: he grew disoriented, agitated, and violent. He set about abusing any and all who gathered around him before lapsing into a coma that brought him to the brink of death.

The court threw serious money at securing the finest seventeenth-century quackery it could buy. These treatments only heightened his suffering: blistering astringents applied to his temples and legs, foot baths full of scalding water, leeches attached to the face, and large doses of opium. Finally, having exhausted all medical know-how, the royal physicians accepted defeat and pronounced him insane, whereupon they called in the "expert" in madness, Doctor Francis Willis. Willis had made a name for himself by setting up an asylum for the insane in Wapping.

In his hands, King George was subjected to many of the standard treatments of the day, including restraint in an iron chair with leg clamps, rope, and a straightjacket. He subjected the King to enforced vomiting, bloodletting, starvation, and cold baths. George's foul-mouthed and incessant ravings were treated with a punitive dismissal: he was tightly gagged. If he appeared restless, or thrashed about in bed feverishly, his legs were tied to the bedposts. Though there were some who quietly disputed the efficacy of this approach, most, including George's sister, Queen Caroline, were complicit. The recognized seventeenth century "cure," after all, was to literally beat the madness out.

Rex nostra insanit

Despite periods of remission, the relapses continued until in 1811 the royal physician confirmed the king's incurable and incessant insanity. By this time, his wife had abandoned him, his eyesight had failed him, and he was completely deaf. He was moved to a far corner of Windsor Castle where he passed his remaining time talking incessantly until hoarse, giving orders to subjects long since dead, and occasionally starting in violent outbursts. He laughed maniacally and continued to undergo the barbarous "cures" of the royal medics. Today, George is assumed to have been a victim of porphyria, a disease characterized by neurological disorder and seizures. At the time, however, no one knew how to treat the condition. As a result, over the last eight years of George's life, the royal household paid what amounted to an astounding £271, 000 for ineffective cures.

Ivan (Antonovich) VI of Russia

(1740–1764)

Born in St. Petersburg, the son of Antony Ulrich of Brunswick-Lüneburg and great-grandson of the feeble-minded Tsar Ivan V of Russia, Ivan become a pawn in the battle for the Russian throne, and as a consequence led a miserable and secluded life, unable to develop in either mind or body.

Baby emperor

At barely eight weeks of age Ivan was adopted by his great-aunt, Empress Anna I of Russia, and named as her successor. A mere twelve days later the Empress died and Ivan became one of the youngest emperors in history. Duke Ernst Johann von Biron was appointed as regent but failed spectacularly in his duties and was arrested after a paltry twenty-two days in office. Ivan's mother (also named Anna) replaced Biron as regent.

A frivolous mother

Anna was an incompetent mother who ignored the baby Ivan while indulging her taste for wild pleasures. She cared nothing for the state of the government, and it came as no surprise that, barely a year later, a revolt by the Russian Imperial Guards overturned the throne and placed upon it instead the daughter of Tsar Peter the Great, Tsarina Elizabeth.

The youngest of prisoners

Ivan and his family were imprisoned. All coins bearing the young tsar's image were removed from circulation, and all paperwork ascertaining his legitimacy to the throne was destroyed. Although locked away, Ivan's mere existence constituted a threat to the usurping monarchy, so he was separated from his family and confined in secrecy in the heavily guarded island fortress of Schlüsselburg.

Barely human

Kept for the remainder of his life in a damp, dark cell, Ivan is thought never to have seen sunlight and was largely kept from having conversations with others. He dressed in filthy rags and was undernourished. His guards would amuse themselves by tormenting him. Solitary confinement kept him from developing emotionally or intellectually.

Escape plot and death

When Catherine the Great came to the throne, she ordered that if anyone were to attempt to release the forgotten tsar, he and his liberator were to be killed. When a lieutenant, Vasily Mirovich, discovered the whereabouts of Ivan he demanded the tsar be handed over and reinstated as emperor. Acting on their instructions, the prison guards immediately murdered the lamentable Ivan and executed his would-be redeemer.

ISABELLA OF BOURBON-PARMA

(1741–1763)

I
sabella of Bourbon-Parma was a shining jewel in the crown of eighteenth-century royalty. Not only was she beautiful, charming, and gentle—she also was possessed of a rare intelligence that helped her to solve complex mathematical problems, consume volumes of French philosophy, and play the violin like an angel. Although she charmed all who met her, she was a melancholic whose obsession with death turned into a morbid neurosis.

Early years

The daughter of Philip, the Duke of Parma, Isabella spent her childhood within the security of her father's court in Madrid and later in Northern Italy. A pretty and delightful child of extraordinary intelligence, she was adored by all around her and grew to be a sophisticated and sensitive young woman. Following her mother's death in 1759, Isabella became prone to bouts of melancholy.

Sisterly love

Isabella was married at age eighteen to Emperor Joseph II of Austria, and although the marriage was motivated by political aspirations, Joseph fell madly in love with his captivating young wife. Isabella charmed the citizens of Vienna, and her grace and intellect resonated magnificently with the polite formalities at court. Isabella, however, was neither particularly fond of her husband nor of the rigid society in which she was now forced to live. Her husband's advances in the bedroom left her disgusted and cold, and she began to spend much of her time with her husband's sister, Marie Christine. Attracted to her sister-in-law's wit, spontaneity, and good looks, it wasn't long before

Isabella became infatuated. The two women spent every waking moment together, laughing, walking, drawing, and playing music. When separated at night, they wrote long and agonized letters to each other declaring their devotion. For Isabella in particular, this obsession took over her life and her marital duties towards her besotted husband became even more distasteful.

The cracks begin to show

Isabella's first pregnancy was difficult and she suffered violent headaches and acute sickness. When the baby was finally delivered, Isabella was dangerously exhausted and spent many weeks confined to her bed. It was during this period that her latent melancholia began to take hold, and Isabella became morbidly obsessed with death. She began to long for death, telling all around her that mortality was a good thing and if she were permitted to kill herself she would. She began hearing voices, and when she suffered two miscarriages in quick succession her condition worsened. She talked of nothing but her impending death.

The end

When Isabella fell pregnant yet again, she was confined to her bed in the hope of preventing another miscarriage. But towards the end of her pregnancy she contracted smallpox and died soon after giving birth to a second daughter.

CHRISTIAN VII
OF DENMARK

(1755–1793)

C hristian VII was a volatile and aggressive drunk with a soft spot for executions. Insane for the duration of his reign, his court succeeded in keeping his mania largely hidden from the public eye.

An unpromising beginning

Christian was the diminutive son of the syphilitic King Frederick V. At the age of two, his mother died and, largely ignored by his father, he was raised by a brutally harsh tutor, whose physical abuse instilled in the young Prince's mind a predilection for self-harm. Not surprisingly he grew increasingly insecure, and sought to compensate for his physical and emotional frailty with violence and aggression.

By his teens he took to prowling the dark streets of Copenhagen with a gang of thugs, carrying spiked clubs with which they would attack at random and ransack shops. He led a debauched life in which he indulged homosexual and sadomasochistic proclivities.

Sado-masochism

It is said that Christian developed a fascination for public executions early in life, and that he attended them regularly, incognito, and staged mock executions in court. He had a rack built for his own personal use, and would insist upon his lover, Conrad Holcke, tying him to it and lashing his back until he drew blood. He loved to inflict burns upon his own skin, and reveled in the pain of rubbing salt into open sores caused through self-mutilation.

Infantile mania

Christian persistently failed to show any interest in the affairs of state. He abandoned his studies and spent his time indulging his childish delight in pranks, throwing food, or attaching upturned pins to his grandmother's chair. When state officials attempted to discuss political issues with him, he would slap their faces, or leapfrog over their backs as they bowed to him.

He married young, to Caroline Mathilda, the sister of George III of England, but went out of his way to make public his distaste for her and for marriage, announcing that he found it "unfashionable to love one's wife." He continued to obsess over whores and had both a mistress and a male lover. Later, the royal physician entrusted with his care, Johann Friedrich Struensee, became the lover of the Queen and, it was rumored, of the King himself. Christian is said to have considered abdication at one point, and to have asked Struensee to elope with him. The Prussian doctor was a man with political aspirations, and without any opposition from the disaffected Christian, he acquired the royal signature on an order that would make him Minister of The Privy Council.

Mental decline

Christian grew ever more delusional, believing himself not to be the rightful Danish King at all, but rather the son of Catherine the Great of Russia. He was either to be found silent and motionless in a far corner of his apartments, or else agitated, ranting, and incomprehensible, running madly about the palace, hurling furniture through windows. His growing paranoia convinced him that he was under siege, and he would demand that his rooms be searched so that hidden assailants could be ousted. Still, the need for self-harm was evident: he would run against walls until his head dripped with blood. At least he was never subjected to barbarous medical treatments, nor confined against his will.

For the last twenty years of his life, he was largely incoherent, though during his brief periods of clarity, he would occasionally be presented to the public, in an attempt to curb the growing rumors in Denmark that the King was being held captive or drugged. Eventually, when the establishment could no longer avoid a public statement, his unusual behavior was attributed to sexual abuse in boyhood by palace page boys. They avoided any reference to madness. He ceased to have any genuine hand in ruling his nation beginning in 1772 and died of a brain aneurysm at age fifty-nine.

MARIE ANTOINETTE
OF FRANCE

(1755–1793)

Marie Antoinette was a vacuous spendthrift who detested all political discussion to such an extent that she was ignorant of the suffering of the people over whom she governed. She indulged in petty extravagances and was widely rumored to have been sexually promiscuous as a young queen. Increasing personal and political tragedies drove her to a clinical depression that never lifted before her execution by guillotine.

Torn from the nest

Maria Antonia, as the Austrian princess was born, found herself betrothed to the Dauphin of France at the age of fourteen. As soon as the arrangements had been finalized, she was given a hasty lesson in French customs and etiquette and made to bid farewell forever to her mother, her home, and her country. The traumatic impact of this departure is well documented and it was a distraught young girl who set off for France.

Her delicate mental state was further tested upon her arrival at the French border. Typical of the extravagant rituals she would soon have to endure at the French court, she was not allowed to set foot on French soil until she had symbolically rid herself of her mother country first.

She was made to part first with her entourage, both staff and companions. Her possessions and her clothing were also to be cast off. Naked and completely alone, she was required to walk through a specially constructed pavilion which straddled the border. Finally, even her name was to be discarded, and from this point on, she became known as Marie Antoinette.

A traumatic transition to womanhood

Her fiancé, the Dauphin Louis XVI, was an immature fifteen-year-old, introverted and intensely shy. Marie Antoinette, already overwhelmed, was married within hours of her arrival in the French court.

The teenagers' union was celebrated with a vast and extravagant public feast, followed by the public blessing of the nuptial bed, to which they were escorted by the entire court. Little wonder then that the sexually inexpert Louis was entirely ill-equipped to consummate the marriage. This situation continued for another seven years.

For those seven years, Marie Antoinette was hounded and tormented by the hushed gossip of aristocratic courtiers, the republican pamphleteers, and even by the raucous cries of market women. Small wonder that she sought distraction in a variety of private and public excesses.

Everything to excess

Marie Antoinette didn't actually respond to news of her people's dire bread shortage and growing famine with instructions to "Let them eat cake." However, she pursued a rigid policy of shunning anything of a sober nature, from the wholly political, to the vaguely serious. No one in her tight clique was permitted to discuss anything except gossip, intrigue, or scandal of a strictly vacuous nature. Consequently she cannot have had any real awareness of the plight of the people living outside the palace walls.

At the same time, she pursued an indulgent and ostentatious lifestyle. She began to spend vast sums of money on her interests and projects: diamonds, gambling, decorating a small palace all her own in the grounds of Versailles. The outward signs of her growing indulgence were clear for all to see: her legendary coiffure grew ever larger and more bizarre, with her vast wigs adorned with priceless jewels, birds, fruit, and flowers.

She surrounded herself with a very select few and shunned senior and respectable aristocrats at court. Her unpopularity with royalists grew almost as fast as it did with republicans.

Exposure, ridicule, and scandal

French custom dictated that few aspects of a queen's life could occur in private. As long as they appeared in respectable costume, anyone could turn up as a spectator to watch the king and queen eat. Furthermore, her toilette was open house for the privileged few curious enough to watch her put on her wig or rouge. Marie Antoinette detested these public exhibitions and her letters back to Austria were testament to her intensifying distress. But the occasion of the very public delivery of her first baby, witnessed by hundreds of eager courtiers, inflicted an entirely new degree of anguish and triggered fainting fits that were to become a growing feature of her ill-fated future.

Meanwhile her unpopularity grew. Her secret excursions to the opera and to balls, dressed in disguise, did nothing to help quash rumors. But a series of pamphlets were published in Paris, highlighting her penchant for sexual deviancy. The fog of propaganda notwithstanding, it is certain that her lavish lifestyle, three-day-long gambling sprees, and exclusive networks of elite companions did not necessarily exclude such proclivities.

Disaster and decline

In spite of everything, Marie Antoinette was a devoted mother. There-
fore the death of her youngest daughter, followed swiftly by the slow
demise of her son from consumption in 1789, marked a significant shift
in her mental health. She grew listless, detached, and disengaged from
life. When republicans seized her husband and condemned him to
death in January 1793, she never fully recovered. She suffered a debilitating nervous breakdown. Her fainting fits worsened, she had frequent
convulsions, and she lost her appetite. She grew emaciated and prema-
turely aged, so that at her own trial later that same year (at which she
was accused of numerous crimes, including incest and sexual assault
upon her own son), her changed appearance shocked those present.

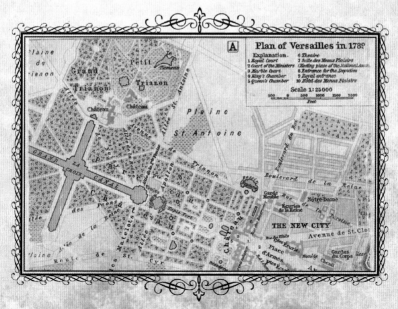

CAROLINE OF BRUNSWICK

(1768–1821)

C aroline of Brunswick was the raving, raucous, and sexually voracious wife of her cousin, George IV of England. Their brief, ill-matched, and ill-fated marriage, followed by a long and scandalous period of separation, fascinated her English subjects, and culminated in a spectacular display of distinctly unroyal behavior upon the occasion of the coronation of her husband.

A match made in heaven?

As a young prince, George had no shortage of female distraction. He had both a lover and an illicit wife by the age of twenty-three. His marriage to the widow Maria Anne Fitzherbert was illegal on two counts: she was a Catholic, which was intolerable under British law; and George married her without seeking his father's permission (presumably since he knew it wouldn't be granted it in any case). Nevertheless, the couple lived happily together for eight years.

George was incurably extravagant and at the end of this eight-year period he had accumulated debts amounting to £630,000. Parliament bargained with him: marry legally, and to an eligible and suitable candidate, and they would absolve his debts. How could he refuse?

Marital bliss

The "eligible" bacheloress selected for him was Caroline. George was appalled by her and reportedly drank steadily after their first meeting until the day of the royal wedding, whereupon he collapsed in a drunken stupor in the bedroom fireplace. The diplomat who accompanied Caroline from Brunswick also took an instant dislike to her, describing her as having "no strong innate notions of [the] value and necessity [of an acquired morality]," along with a particularly large head.

Although George had been forced into giving up his first "wife," he had no intention of dumping his mistress, whom he brought with him on the honeymoon. Somehow, he put aside his aversion to Caroline's neglectful hygiene and coarse vulgarity long enough to impregnate her early in their marriage, whereupon he wrote her a letter announcing their formal separation.

Indecent exposure

Caroline began partying to excess, satisfied her voracious sexuality on a regular basis, and developed a taste for exposing herself in public which was only to grow more marked as the years went by. In the Georgian court, such untrammeled impropriety was too shocking to be permitted to continue. Caroline soon found herself the subject of serious court intrigue when it was claimed that she had given birth to an illegitimate son. The proceedings were known as "The Delicate Investigation," although there was little delicacy involved and Caroline's name was disgraced.

She fled England, vowing never to return, and settled in France and Italy, where she had a scandalous and open affair first with Napoleon's brother-in-law and then with his courtier.

The return of Queen Caroline

Her determination to shun England forever lasted only until news reached her of the death of her father-in-law, King George III. Realizing this meant her husband would finally be crowned King, England no longer seemed such an unattractive prospect, and so she returned, determined to take up her throne.

Appalled by the public relations disaster that she represented, Parliament attempted to secure a royal divorce prior to the coronation. Once more, Caroline was subjected to a very public and humiliating exposure of her sex life, but this time Londoners rallied to her support. Every day her coach was escorted to court by a chanting mob. The power of the people was sufficient to sway Parliament, and the divorce was never granted.

A right royal fiasco

All of Caroline's attempts to prepare herself for her coronation were blocked and ignored. Infuriated, George was determined she should not participate. Undeterred, Caroline turned up at doors of Westminster Abbey on the day of the coronation, only to find them locked.

Dressed appallingly and foregoing any last shred of decorum, she hollered and hammered on the doors, demanding entry. Her pleas were not heeded.

She died weeks later, wretched and humiliated.

141

FERDINAND I OF AUSTRIA

(1793–1875)

F erdinand I of Austria was a gentle soul who spent his reign shuffling around in a state of shambolic puzzlement, barely able to string two words together, let alone understand the politics of his country. As a descendant of the inbred Hapsburg line, it was no surprise that he turned out to be a monstrous genetic mutation.

Kissing cousins

Ferdinand was the second-born child of Emperor Franz II of Austria and his second wife and cousin, Marie Therese of Naples. Born with a hugely swollen head (due to hydrocephalus), a vast protuberance for a nose, the famous Hapsburg drooping lower lip, and a dull and vacant expression, the young Ferdinand was a disastrous reminder of the hazards of royal inbreeding.

A royal embarrassment

Despite all best efforts and the finest of tutors, Ferdinand's physical and mental condition did not improve. He was unable to hold a cup steady, so could not feed himself, and after years of expert tutelage he was barely able to write his own name or string together an intelligible sentence. His frequent epileptic fits required that he be kept out of public view. Nevertheless, upon his father's death, he acquired the Imperial Crown of Austria.

Dumplings

As Emperor, Ferdinand was incompetent, and a regent's council was appointed to steer the government. The only sentence he ever uttered which could be entirely understood was, "I am the Emperor, and I want dumplings."

Bride of Frankenstein

As surprising as it seems, it was deemed necessary for a bride to be chosen for the oafish Emperor in the ludicrous hope that he could sire an heir. Ferdinand is reported to have suffered five epileptic fits on their wedding night, and the hapless union likely never was consummated. Maria Anna became his nurse and stood by his side when his fits became more frequent and his health diminished.

A contented old age

Despite everything, Ferdinand was a popular monarch who was looked on with affection by his subjects, not least because, while out walking, he was in the habit of giving away every possession he had on him to random passers-by. When economic depression and rebellion threatened the country it was obvious something had to be done, and so Ferdinand was forced to abdicate in favor of his nephew, Franz Joseph. It was the beginning of a happy ending for Ferdinand, who moved to Prague with his wife and lived in contentment, surrounded by his collection of heraldry, till the ripe old age of eighty-two.

Franz Joseph I of Austria

CHARLOTTE OF BELGIUM

(1840–1927)

C harlotte was a beautiful and intelligent woman who was deeply in love with her husband and worked alongside him dutifully in Mexico. But he was a wayward husband, and the pressure from her deteriorating personal life, along with the venereal disease with which he had infected her, and their tentative and unpopular tenure in Mexico, ultimately sent Charlotte raving mad.

Fairy-tale romance

When Charlotte first met the handsome and idealistic Archduke Maximilian, brother to the Austrian Emperor, the couple fell instantly in love. Young, intelligent, and with striking good looks, they were well suited to each other. But Maximilian's youthful exuberance was not something he was prepared to relinquish simply because he had now gained himself a wife. He continued to indulge in sexual relations with whomever he chose. Charlotte was prepared to tolerate his indiscretions only until she discovered she had contracted syphilis from him. Distraught, she refused ever to share a bed with him again.

A working relationship

Charlotte however, remained loyal and committed to her husband and when Napoleon III of France offered him the exalted position of Emperor of Mexico, she urged him to accept. Together, they worked hard to make their new crown a success. The strain on her was immeasurable: by day she would draw up affairs of state for her husband, and appear in public as the perfect royal spouse; at night Maximilian preferred the company of his teenage mistress.

The first public signs that the pressure of this double life was beginning to show came in 1866. Napoleon had decided to withdraw his financial support for their Mexican crown. Charlotte traveled back to Europe to plead with Napoleon and with the Pope. Already nervous and depressed, her failure to win over either man caused a complete emotional breakdown: on both occasions she became hysterical, causing Pope Pius IX to remark, "nothing is spared me in this life: now a woman has to go mad in the Vatican!"

Encroaching madness

Charlotte grew increasingly paranoid, refusing all food and telling the Pope that she was being poisoned. Her behavior grew ever more erratic: her conviction that her servants were attempting to poison her food led her to insist that any chickens given for her to dine upon had first to be slaughtered in her presence.

She was ushered away to the privacy of her Italian home, and never to set foot in Mexico again. Her paranoia worsened, possibly because of a syphilitic condition. She hid her face when traveling and saw no one.

News that her husband had been executed by a firing squad in Mexico in 1867 proved the breaking point. Her family removed her to a private palace in Belgium where she lived in seclusion for the rest of days. She had periods of lucidity, during which she wrote letters and read copiously. Her appearance never suffered: she remained a striking woman, but her bouts of insanity were destructive and consuming. She would smash and break objects around her, insist that she was still in Mexico, and sleep with a doll that she spoke to, calling it Max. In all her hysterical rages, she never once broke anything that had belonged to her husband.

LUDWIG II "THE SWAN KING" OF BAVARIA

(1845–1886)

L udwig II was an eccentric fantasist obsessed with the music of Richard Wagner and the regal beauty of the majestic swans that floated serenely on the nearby waters of Swan Lake. A latent homosexual, Ludwig II lived a guilt-ridden life which ended tragically when he was found drowned under mysterious circumstances three days after being declared insane.

A repressed childhood

Ludwig's early life was certainly not ideal. A traumatic birth was followed by the death of his wet-nurse and inadequate parenting from a mother and father who had no understanding of children. Extravagantly spoiled and constantly reminded of the importance of his royal position, Ludwig grew to be haughty and introverted. A series of strict and unforgiving tutors caused him to withdraw into his own secretive world of fantasies as a means to survive. He began to experience hallucinations at the age of fourteen.

Guilty pleasures

Young and inexperienced, Ludwig ascended to the throne at the age of eighteen, surprising the government with his ruthless determination to have his own way in all matters.

Pressure to produce an heir ended when Ludwig called off his extended engagement to his cousin, Sophie. He never married, preferring instead the company of handsome young men: artists and actors were drawn to the King's brooding good looks and poetic nature. A committed Catholic, Ludwig could never reconcile his sexual urges with his religious beliefs, and spent his days tortured by guilt.

Building castles in the air

Increasingly withdrawn and obsessive, Ludwig began to isolate himself in the Alps, indulging all his wildest fantasies. Using his personal fortune he constructed castles of breathtaking imagination on the most grandiose and preposterous scale. Neuschwanstein Castle was inspired by his love of Wagner and his opera Lohengrin, with its famous swan-knight hero. Ludwig had the castle painted with flamboyant scenes from the opera and filled with all manner of swan icons. Other castles were decked out with scenes from Arabia, and Ludwig would imagine himself a Turkish Sultan, all his needs seen to by a harem of half-naked solider boys.

A mysterious ending

The government finally tired of Ludwig's antics, and in 1886 he was declared insane, placed under arrest, and taken to the Castle Berg. Based on the testimonies of a number of servants and government officials, Ludwig was diagnosed with paranoia before he was even seen by the acting psychiatrist, Professor Bernhard von Gudden. Three days after his arrest, Ludwig requested an evening walk along the shores of a nearby lake. He was accompanied by Professor Gudden and the two men were found dead in the water later the same night. Ludwig's death was declared a suicide by drowning, even though he was known to be a good swimmer.

APPENDIX I: Mad Monarchs by Nationality

(With dates of reign)

British Monarchs

Robert III of Scotland 1390–1406
Henry VIII of England 1509–1547
George III of England 1760–1820

German Monarchs

Anna of Saxony 1561–1575
Maria Eleonore of Brandenburg 1620–1632
Frederick William I of Prussia 1713–1740
Caroline of Brunswick 1820–1821
Ludwig II "The Swan King" of Bavaria 1864–1886

Scandinavian Monarchs

Erik XIV of Sweden 1560–1568
Christina of Sweden 1632–1654
Christian VII of Denmark 1766–1808

French Monarchs

Isabella "She-Wolf" of France 1308–1327
Charles VI of France 1380–1422
Louis XIV of France 1643–1715
Marie Antoinette of France 1755–1793

Italian Monarchs

Joan I of Naples 1343–1382
Gian Gastone de' Medici 1723–1737
Isabella of Bourbon-Parma 1760–1763

Portuguese Monarchs

Isabel of Portugal 1447–1454
Barbara of Portugal 1746–1758
Maria I of Portugal 1777–1816

Spanish Monarchs

Juana of Castile 1504–1555
Charles II of Spain 1665–1700
Philip V of Spain 1700–1746
Ferdinand VI of Spain 1746–1759

Belgian Monarchs

Charlotte of Belgium 1864–1867

Austrio-Hungarian Monarchs

Rudolf II of Austria 1576–1612
Ferdinand I of Austria 1835–1848

Russian Monarchs

Ivan "The Terrible" of Russia 1547–1584
Fyodor I "The Bellringer" of Russia 1584–1598
Ivan "The Ignorant" of Russia 1682–1696
Peter the Great of Russia 1682–1725
Anna I of Russia 1730–1740
Catherine the Great of Russia 1762–1796
Ivan (Antonovich) VI of Russia 1740–1741

Balkan Monarchs

Vlad "The Impaler" of Walachia 1448; 1456–62; 1476
Erzsébet Báthory of Hungary 1575–1614

Turkish Monarchs

Mustafa I of Turkey 1617–1618; 1622–1623
Murad IV of Turkey 1623–1640
Ibrahim I of Turkey 1640–1648

APPENDIX II:
ROYAL LINEAGES

In the following royal lineages, only those monarchs who can be shown to have close family ties have been featured.

HOUSE OF VALOIS
France

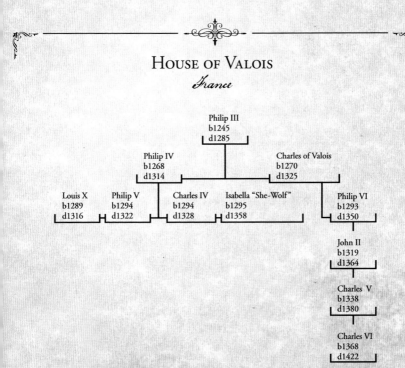

Philip III
b1245
d1285

Philip IV
b1268
d1314

Charles of Valois
b1270
d1325

Louis X
b1289
d1316

Philip V
b1294
d1322

Charles IV
b1294
d1328

Isabella "She-Wolf"
b1295
d1358

Philip VI
b1293
d1350

John II
b1319
d1364

Charles V
b1338
d1380

Charles VI
b1368
d1422

The House of Romanov
Russia

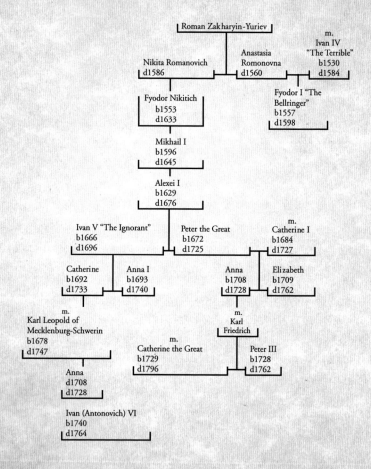

Roman Zakharyin-Yuriev

Nikita Romanovich
d1586

Anastasia
Romonovna
d1560

m.
Ivan IV
"The Terrible"
b1530   d1584

Fyodor Nikitich
b1553
d1633

Fyodor I "The
Bellringer"
b1557
d1598

Mikhail I
b1596
d1645

Alexei I
b1629
d1676

Ivan V "The Ignorant"
b1666
d1696

Peter the Great
b1672
d1725

m.
Catherine I
b1684
d1727

Catherine
b1692
d1733

Anna I
b1693
d1740

Anna
b1708
d1728

Elizabeth
b1709
d1762

m.
Karl Leopold of
Mecklenburg-Schwerin
b1678
d1747

m.
Karl
Friedrich

m.
Catherine the Great
b1729
d1796

Peter III
b1728
d1762

Anna
d1708
d1728

Ivan (Antonovich) VI
b1740
d1764

HOUSES OF WASA AND HOHENZOLLERN
Sweden and Prussia

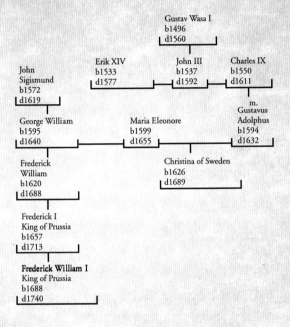

Gustav Wasa I
b1496
d1560

John
Sigismund
b1572
d1619

Erik XIV
b1533
d1577

John III
b1537
d1592

Charles IX
b1550
d1611

m.
Gustavus
Adolphus
b1594
d1632

George William
b1595
d1640

Maria Eleonore
b1599
d1655

Christina of Sweden
b1626
d1689

Frederick
William
b1620
d1688

Frederick I
King of Prussia
b1657
d1713

Frederick William I
King of Prussia
b1688
d1740

HOUSE OF BOURBON
Spain, Portugal, and France

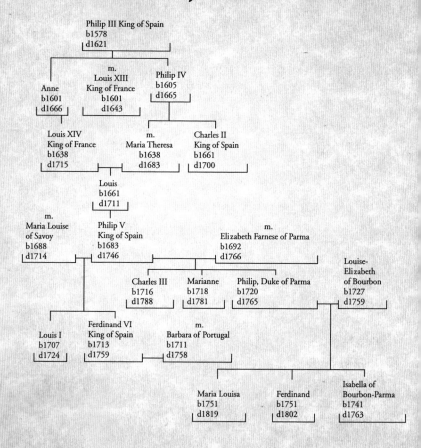

Philip III King of Spain
b1578
d1621

Anne
b1601
d1666

m.
Louis XIII
King of France
b1601
d1643

Philip IV
b1605
d1665

Louis XIV
King of France
b1638
d1715

m.
Maria Theresa
b1638
d1683

Charles II
King of Spain
b1661
d1700

Louis
b1661
d1711

m.
Maria Louise
of Savoy
b1688
d1714

Philip V
King of Spain
b1683
d1746

m.
Elizabeth Farnese of Parma
b1692
d1766

Louise-
Elizabeth
of Bourbon
b1727
d1759

Charles III
b1716
d1788

Marianne
b1718
d1781

Philip, Duke of Parma
b1720
d1765

Louis I
b1707
d1724

Ferdinand VI
King of Spain
b1713
d1759

m.
Barbara of Portugal
b1711
d1758

Maria Louisa
b1751
d1819

Ferdinand
b1751
d1802

Isabella of
Bourbon-Parma
b1741
d1763

House of Hapsburg
Spain, Portugal, and Austria-Hungary

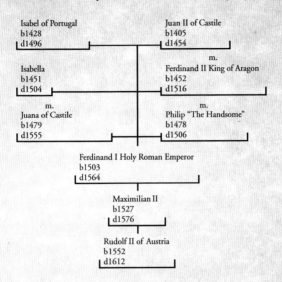

Isabel of Portugal
b1428
d1496

Juan II of Castile
b1405
d1454

Isabella
b1451
d1504

m.
Ferdinand II King of Aragon
b1452
d1516

m.
Juana of Castile
b1479
d1555

m.
Philip "The Handsome"
b1478
d1506

Ferdinand I Holy Roman Emperor
b1503
d1564

Maximilian II
b1527
d1576

Rudolf II of Austria
b1552
d1612

Ottoman Sultans
Turkey

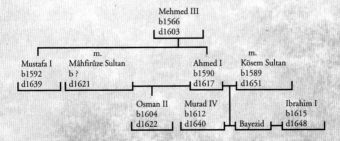

Mehmed III
b1566
d1603

Mustafa I
b1592
d1639

m.
Mâhfirûze Sultan
b ?
d1621

Ahmed I
b1590
d1617

m.
Kösem Sultan
b1589
d1651

Osman II
b1604
d1622

Murad IV
b1612
d1640

Bayezid

Ibrahim I
b1615
d1648

THE HOUSE OF HANOVER
England, Germany, and Denmark

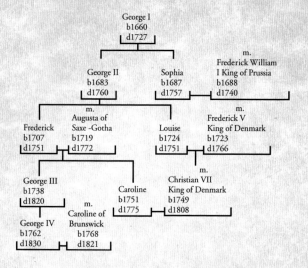

George I
b1660
d1727

George II
b1683
d1760

m.
Augusta of
Saxe -Gotha
b1719
d1772

Sophia
b1687
d1757

m.
Frederick William
I King of Prussia
b1688
d1740

Frederick
b1707
d1751

Louise
b1724
d1751

m.
Frederick V
King of Denmark
b1723
d1766

George III
b1738
d1820

Caroline
b1751
d1775

Christian VII
King of Denmark
b1749
d1808

m.
Caroline of
Brunswick
b1768
d1821

George IV
b1762
d1830